MACMILLAN MASTER GUIDES

SENSE AND SENSIBILITY

BY JANE AUSTEN

JUDY SIMONS

**MACMILLAN
EDUCATION**

First edition 1987

Published by
MACMILLAN EDUCATION LTD
Houndmills, Basingstoke, Hampshire RG21 2XS
and London
Companies and representatives
throughout the world

Printed in Hong Kong

British Library Cataloguing in Publication Data
Simons, Judy,
Sense and sensibility by Jane Austen.—
(Macmillan master guides)
1. Austen, Jane. Sense and sensibility
I. Title
823'.7   PR4037
ISBN 0-333-42164-7 Pbk
ISBN 0-333-42165-5 Pbk export

Cover illustration: *Arranging flowers* by Edmund Bundy. Photo-
graph © Eaton Gallery and by courtesy of Bridgeman Art Library.

CONTENTS

GENERAL EDITOR'S PREFACE

The aim of the Macmillan Master Guides is to help you to appreciate the book you are studying by providing information about it and by suggesting ways of reading and thinking about it will lead to a fuller understanding. The sections on the writer's life and background have been designed to illustrate those aspects of the writer's life which have influenced the work, and to place it in its personal and literary context. The summaries and critical commentary are of special importance in that each brief summary of the action is followed by an examination of the significant critical points. The space which might have been given to repetitive explanatory notes has been devoted to a detailed analysis of the kind of passage which might confront you in an examination. Literary criticism is concerned with both the broader aspects of the work being studied and with its detail. The ideas which meet us in reading a great work of literature, and their relevance to us today, are an essential part of our study, and our Guides look at the thought of their subject in some detail. But just as essential is the craft with which the writer has constructed his work of art, and this may be considered under several technical headings – characterisation, language, style and stagecraft, for example.

The authors of these Guides are all teachers and writers of wide experience, and they have chosen to write about books they admire and know well in the belief that they can communicate their admiration to you. But you yourself must read and know intimately the book you are studying. No one can do that for you. You should see this book as a lamp-post. Use it to shed light, not to lean against. If you know your text and know what it is saying about life, and how it says it, then you will enjoy it, and there is no better way of passing an examination in literature.

JAMES GIBSON

1 JANE AUSTEN: LIFE AND BACKGROUND

Jane Austen was born on the 16 December 1775 in the village of Steventon in Hampshire, where her father was Rector. She was the seventh of eight children and most of her early life was spent at home, where she grew up sheltered and secure. Little is really known about the details of Jane Austen's life, despite some admirable guesswork done by biographers. This is partly because quite a lot of correspondence was destroyed by her family after her death, presumably to conceal any intimate or damaging information. We do know, however, that her father, the Reverend George Austen, and her mother, Cassandra (née Leigh), were caring parents, sensible and well-educated. According to the evidence of the surviving letters, family life at Steventon was united and comfortable. The children were all quite near in age: the eldest was born in 1765, the youngest in 1779 but Jane developed particularly close relationships with her brother Henry who was four years older than herself, and her sister, Cassandra, who was two years older, and whom she adored. 'If Cassandra were going to have her head cut off,' wrote their mother, 'Jane would insist on sharing her fate.' Theirs was an intimacy which was to last throughout Jane's life, and we can see what she felt about sisterly affection and the special closeness it can create when we read *Sense and Sensibility* and the portrayal of the Dashwood girls. The family and what it represents is a subject that dominates most of Jane Austen's novels, and in *Sense and Sensibility* the relationships between sisters and brothers, parents and children, and the influence of more distant relatives, such as Sir John Middleton, are made the pivot for the novel's action. Life in the small village of Steventon was quiet and ordered. Jane Austen's parents were both from the English upper middle class, the class known then as the 'gentry', and it is this class which figures almost exclusively in Jane

Austen's novels. It was a class which could incorporate a range of occupations. Her father's family, for instance, had diverse interests in the professions, in commerce and in landowning, and we can see how this sort of family ramification appears in Jane Austen's works. She often deals with rich and poor members of the same family, and with relatives who rise or sink in social position. Mrs Jennings and her daughters are one example of this in *Sense and Sensibility*.

Mrs Austen's family had a more distinguished history, both socially (one of her ancestors had been Lord Mayor of London in the sixteenth century) and intellectually (her uncle was Master of Balliol College, Oxford). Jane Austen's interest in the activities and status of this upper middle class was fostered too by the eventual careers of her own brothers. Edward, the third son, had been adopted in childhood by a wealthy relative of Mr Austen, Thomas Knight, whose estates he inherited. James, the eldest, went into the Church, and became Rector of Steventon after his father. Henry was first a captain in the Oxford Militia and then a banker before he too opted for the Church as a career, and the other sons, Francis and Charles, went into the Navy, where they both attained the rank of Admiral. As careers for the men in her novels, the Church, the Army and the Navy occur again and again.

When Jane Austen was seven she was sent away with Cassandra to boarding school in Oxford, but after just over a year spent at establishments in Southampton and finally Reading, she returned home, never again to leave the family circle for any length of time. We must not assume from this however, that her education necessarily suffered as a result. In fact at home she probably had much better opportunities for learning than if she had spent her formative years at an academy for young ladies. Both her parents were intelligent and well-read people and had a great respect for learning. Her father was a scholar who took in resident tutorial pupils, and he gave Jane and Cassandra a grounding in the classics. Her brothers also took a strong interest in the girls' education. But the most significant influence on Jane Austen's intellectual development was her exposure to a great range of literature from the classical writers of Greece and Rome to more contemporary authors. She read widely and voraciously, essays, sermons, poetry and plays. She was particularly fond of the writing of the eighteenth-century essayist, Dr Johnson, whose style of reasoned discourse and judgemental analysis had a deeply influential effect on her own artistic career. Most importantly, however, she loved novels, a fairly recent genre in English. Among her favourites were Samuel Richardson's *Sir Charles Grandison* (1753) and the novels of Fanny Burney, which amalgamated their moral interest with a close focus on individual experience, especially female experience. Mr Austen had an extensive library and Jane's use of it was not curtailed as it might have been had she been born in the mid-nineteenth instead of the eighteenth century. Hence we do not find the prudery in Jane Austen that we associate with some later nineteenth-century writers.

Reading fed her imagination and her natural interest in language, and while she was still an adolescent, she began to experiment with different styles of writing and forms of literary composition. Writing letters and keeping lengthy diaries were considered fairly normal pursuits for young women of that time – look at the ways in which letter-writing features in *Sense and Sensibility* for instance – but Jane Austen's talents led her to more elaborate types of experiment. From about the age of twelve, she began to write fiction, drama and even her own version of English history, and her early surviving compositions have been collected and published as her *Juvenilia*. These contain her work from the years 1787–93 and demonstrate above all her immense sense of fun, her verbal fluency and her keen ear for the ridiculous. Her enjoyment of the absurd found a wonderful source of satire in the far-fetched romantic novels which flooded the market in the late eighteenth century. Her interest in literary parody never faded, and although her early exuberance was toned down as her art matured, elements of burlesque can be found to some degree in all her work.

During the years 1794–9, Jane Austen wrote the major part of her first three novels, which were to be published later as *Sense and Sensibility* (1811), *Pride and Prejudice* (1813) and *Northanger Abbey* (1818). The rectory at Steventon was a noisy place and conditions there were not particularly conducive to sustained literary production. Jane Austen's days were filled with household chores, social visits and family affairs, the concerns indeed that form the substance of her fiction. She had little opportunity for privacy. She didn't even have a bedroom to herself, but shared one with her sister, Cassandra. We know that when she was engaged in writing, she expected to be continually interrupted, and that she wrote her novels on single sheets of paper so that her work could be easily hidden away out of sight if she were disturbed.

In 1801, her father retired from the position of Rector and announced one day, apparently out of the blue, that the family would be moving to Bath. The news came as a great shock to Jane Austen, to whom stability was always of the utmost importance, and apparently she fainted when she heard that she was to leave Steventon. It is too easy to assume that she fainted because she had a genteel lady's propensity for swooning, but it is more likely that she was already suffering from Addison's Disease, an illness which among other effects reduces the capacity of the body to cope with stress, and which ultimately was to kill her. Jane Austen was unhappy in Bath, where she lived until her father's death in 1805. She never liked cities, but preferred a quiet, rural existence. The places of greatest harmony in her novels are always to be found in country villages. Urban life in general is treated critically. *Sense and Sensibility* portrays London as a city of meretricious glamour, shallow and materialistic. Bath itself appears in *Northanger Abbey* and, with greater bitterness, in *Persuasion* as an essentially temporary place, its inhabitants rootless and bored.

After her father's death, Jane Austen, Cassandra and their mother, with some financial help from her brothers, eventually settled at Chawton, another Hampshire village, near her brother Edward's estate. It was here that Jane Austen was to live until her death, and here that her next three novels were written, *Mansfield Park* (1814), *Emma* (1815) and *Persuasion* (published posthumously in 1818). She also began work on a novel that she was never to complete, *Sanditon*. The years spent at Chawton were happy and settled ones, and in an environment of permanence and untroubled affection, Jane Austen's creative energies could flourish. It was during this time that she began actively to seek publication. She revised *Sense and Sensibility* which had started life as a novel in letters, entitled *Elinor and Marianne*, and it was sent to Thomas Egerton, a London publisher. It appeared as a three volume novel in November 1811, priced at fifteen shillings, and as it was published anonymously as being only 'By a lady', Jane Austen was able to keep her identity as authoress secret from all except her immediate family. The sales were encouraging, so much so that she embarked on revising the work she had called

First Impressions and which was published as *Pride and Prejudice* shortly over a year later. Jane Austen was never famous in her own lifetime – the celebrity of Fanny Burney was far greater – but by the time she came to write *Emma*, the secret of her authorship had been leaked. She was considered something of a success and as a mark of favour she was invited to dedicate that novel to the Prince Regent who was an admirer of her work. In her last years, she continued to write (*Persuasion*) and to revise (*Susan* became *Northanger Abbey*), but unfortunately the illness from which she was suffering gradually sapped her strength, and although she fought it with a resilient spirit, there was no known cure. She went to lodge in Winchester in order to be near her doctor, but on the 18 July 1817, aged forty-one, she died in Cassandra's arms. She was buried in Winchester Cathedral.

It is often tempting to think of Jane Austen's life as a narrow one and to assume from this that her interests were similarly narrow. Certainly it is true that Jane Austen never married, nor had children of her own. To the best of our knowledge she had only one brief love affair and that ended tragically. She lived quietly, her activities confined to the circle of her family and a few friends, and she travelled little. Students often complain that her novels ignore the problems of her age because they do not describe the living conditions of the working classes nor enquire into the views of servants. We make a great mistake if we equate the events of her life with a corresponding limitation of vision.

Firstly, we need to remember that Jane Austen grew up in the eighteenth century. Because her writing is often more accessible to modern readers than that of her contemporaries, we tend to place her side by side with authors of a much later date. Jane Austen was a product of her time, a time before the concern with humanitarian issues figured large in the public consciousness. Topics such as class injustice, poverty and industrialism tended to become dominant interests only in the Victorian era. But Jane Austen was acutely alert to the climate of her age and its implications. It is important to realise that her choice of artistic material was a deliberate one. She knew what she was doing when she decided to write 'three or four families in a country village', as she once described her novels' subjects. Yet from this unpromising matter, she was able to envisage some fundamental principles of social organisation and to comment on them. She had a sociologist's eye for recognising the wider movements within a social structure and she saw what happened in her own immediate circle as symptomatic of large-scale historical processes. So, in her novels, Jane Austen presents us with a picture of a society in flux, where the forces of free enterprise are often in conflict with the traditions of an established aristocracy. Her later Chawton novels in particular reflect this shift, but her earlier ones too show her awareness of class mobility. If we read her books carefully, we can identify too a firm basis for a critique of society, and discover in her realistic approach to specific issues a more universal application.

Throughout her life, Jane Austen was surrounded by the spirit of revolution in its political, social and cultural manifestations. All had a deep impact on her perception of things. She was born just before the American War of Independence, when the American states discarded their colonial status and fought against England for their right to self-government. She lived through the disturbed times of the French Revolution and saw its effects at first hand when her cousin Eliza, who had married a French nobleman, fled the French Terror and came to Steventon as a refugee. During Jane Austen's lifetime, English society was changing as the industrial revolution made its effects felt. She saw the growth of towns, the subsequent population shifts and an increased ease of transport and communication systems. For much of her adult life, too, England was a country at war. If these events do not appear directly in her novels, they do provide a context of unrest in which her fiction is set.

But it was the cultural revolution which was perhaps the most pervasive in its effect on her thinking. On the one hand, the eighteenth century had been known as the 'Age of Reason', where the attitudes of the 'enlightenment' emphasised man's capacity for understanding the world according to rational principles. On the other hand, the latter years of the century saw the growth of Romanticism which gave credence to man's intuition and spontaneous affections as a reliable guide for action. Jane Austen's own creative period was exactly parallel with that of some of the greatest English Romantic writers, William Wordsworth, Samuel Taylor Coleridge and Sir Walter Scott. It was a time of intense intellectual ferment and Jane Austen's work is informed by a complex background of ideological debate.

The tension between Classicism (the philosophy based on an ordered rationalism) and Romanticism (the philosophy based on personal feeling), which pervaded much contemporary debate, is a tension reflected in Jane Austen's own writing, as she examines the problematic relationship between the system and the individual. It penetrates her view of a whole range of contemporary issues; of, for instance, the distribution of wealth, of the idea of a social hierarchy and its determinants, and of her attitude to the status of women in the social framework. One of the problems for us in reading *Sense and Sensibility* is our distance from the eighteenth-century literature it refers to. Clearly, the novel goes beyond mere burlesque, but we need to know that Jane Austen was in the business of poking fun at particular literary conventions. When she uses the terms *sense* and *sensibility*, for instance, she does so with a strong sense of their contemporary application. In part, the words themselves reflect the division between 'reason' and 'romanticism', but we must be careful not to try to interpret them too simply or to assume that they define merely the opposition between 'head' and 'heart'. The concepts they embody are complex and are used by Jane Austen with different levels of meaning. By *sense* she does mean primarily a respect for order, logic and rational control. This can take the form of balanced impartiality, or in its extreme form could manifest itself as callousness or rigidity.

Sensibility is more complicated. It involves not only the idea of emotional sensitivity but also an excess of self-awareness. By the time Jane Austen came to write *Sense and Sensibility*, sensibility had become something of a literary cult. Its devotees, known as sentimentalists, prided themselves on being more delicate than their fellow beings. They made a virtue out of being able to respond instinctively to affecting situations, often quite trivial ones, and the display of extreme emotion on these occasions was thought to indicate the possession of a feeling heart, in itself reckoned to be a sufficient moral guide. Marianne Dashwood's farewells are a good example of disproportionate emotion exhibited in an everyday situation. Pleasure was to be found in the contemplation of melancholy subjects and, in emphasising the values of individual experience at the expense of all else, sentimentalists sought out opportunities for introspection and isolation.

The beauty of natural scenery was greatly admired because it was a living example of spiritual freedom, growth that had not been inhibited by any imposed system.

In this context, one further term that perhaps requires explanation is the term 'picturesque'. In *Sense and Sensibility*, this refers to a specific theory about artistic principles, which compared the appreciation of scenic beauty with the appreciation of painting. Contemporary theories of composition and harmony and visual effects are mocked in Marianne's failure to apply them properly, but they also become a fundamental pointer in our reading of a book which examines the relationship between art and nature as one of its pervasive themes.

2 SUMMARIES AND CRITICAL COMMENTARY

2.1 OVERALL PLOT SYNOPSIS

After their father's death, Elinor and Marianne Dashwood are forced to move with their mother and young sister, Margaret, away from their family home in order to make way for the new owner, their half-brother John and his wife, Fanny. They move to Barton cottage on the estate of Sir John Middleton, a cousin of Mrs Dashwood's. Soon after they arrive, the pretty and vivacious Marianne falls in love with the dashing John Willoughby, heir to a neighbouring estate. She also attracts the attention of an older, quieter man who is a guest at Barton, Colonel Brandon, but ignores him. Meanwhile, her elder sister, Elinor, silently nurses her own love for Edward Ferrars, Fanny Dashwood's brother.

Despite the evident growing affection between Marianne and Willoughby, no engagement is announced and, much to Marianne's obvious distress, Willoughby leaves Barton not saying when he will return. The subsequent tedium of days is broken by the arrival of two sisters, Lucy and Anne Steele, who come to visit the Middletons. Elinor and Marianne take an instant dislike to them, but are thrown constantly into their company. After a few days, Lucy Steele confides to Elinor that she has been secretly engaged to Edward Ferrars for the past three years. Elinor is deeply shocked at this disclosure and is convinced that Edward does not love Lucy, but she tells no-one.

Mrs Jennings, Lady Middleton's mother, invites Elinor and Marianne to accompany her to London for the winter season. Elinor is reluctant to accept, afraid that she might meet Edward there, but Marianne, hoping to re-encounter Willoughby, is enthusiastic about the offer and Mrs Dashwood encourages them to accept. In London, Marianne is morose until one evening she espies Willoughby at an evening party. She greets him with delight but he publicly snubs her and she has to be taken home, ill. The next day she hears that Willoughby is engaged to be married to a Miss Grey, a wealthy heiress.

John and Fanny Dashwood, who are also in town, invite the Steele sisters to stay, hoping to prevent any renewal of the intimacy they suspect existed between Elinor and Edward. To their dismay and the horror of Fanny's snobbish mother, Mrs Ferrars, Anne Steele inadvertently discloses the fact of the romance between Edward and her sister Lucy. The Steeles are evicted unceremoniously from the house and Mrs Ferrars disinherits Edward in favour of her younger son, Robert. Colonel Brandon, hearing of events, asks Elinor to speak to Edward on his behalf, offering him the vacant living on his estate at Delaford, a position which would bring in enough income to enable Edward to marry Lucy. As they are about to leave London for Barton, Elinor and Marianne hear the news of Willoughby's wedding.

En route for home the sisters break their journey at Cleveland, the home of Mrs Palmer, Mrs Jennings' other daughter. While there, Marianne catches a cold which turns feverish and she becomes dangerously ill. Colonel Brandon, who has accompanied the Palmers, goes to fetch Mrs Dashwood, and while alone in the house, nursing her sister through the crisis, Elinor is visited by Willoughby who, torn by remorse and believing Marianne close to death, comes to explain his conduct. Despite herself, Elinor warms to him. Marianne recovers and the girls return to Barton, both saddened by their experiences. Some weeks later they hear that Lucy's marriage has taken place, but their despondency at the news is soon relieved by the appearance of Edward himself who announces that Lucy has in fact eloped with his brother Robert, and that he is now freed from his unhappy entanglement. Elinor and Edward are married and move to Delaford parsonage. In time, recovering from her first passion for Willoughby, a more mature Marianne finds that she comes to love Colonel Brandon and they too are happily married.

2.2 INTRODUCTION

When *Sense and Sensibility* was first printed in 1811, it was divided
into three volumes, each of which began numbering from Chapter
1. The first volume contained twenty-two chapters, and the second
and third volumes fourteen chapters each. The chapter numbering
referred to throughout this Masterguide, however, is that found in
most current twentieth-century editions of the text, numbering
consecutively from Chapter 1 to Chapter 50. You will probably
find this the simplest and most readily available numbering
system.

The text that I have used is that published by Macmillan in the
Macmillan Students Novels series, edited by Raymond Wilson,
but any text would be just as acceptable.

2.3 CHAPTER SUMMARIES AND COMMENTARIES

Chapter 1
Mr Henry Dashwood has inherited a grand estate, Norland, only
to find that in the terms of the will, the accompanying fortune must
be left intact to John, his son by his first marriage, with nothing for
his present wife and their three daughters. His untimely death thus
leaves Mrs Dashwood, Elinor (nineteen), Marianne (seventeen)
and Margaret (thirteen) with a very meagre income. The level-
headed Elinor and the impulsive Marianne are briefly described.
With Marianne and her mother prostrate with grief after Mr
Dashwood's death, the practical arrangements of welcoming the
heir to Norland are left to Elinor.

Commentary
This apparently simple opening chapter, written in an almost
dismissive style, in fact introduces several of the complexities and
subtle oppositions which characterise this novel. By giving the
immediate family history, Jane Austen emphasises the conditions
which determine the Dashwoods' lives, and the elements of chance
involved (note that the property is bequeathed to John on a whim
of sentiment for his baby son). Moral contrasts are set up between
the selfish John and Fanny Dashwood and the sensitive Mrs
Dashwood and her daughters. These have wide-reaching implica-

tions, for sensitivity is no guarantee of income and the Dashwood women are not rewarded for their virtues. The theme of *sense and sensibility* is introduced as we move from the callous common *sense* of Fanny (Mrs John) Dashwood via the balanced restraint of Elinor to the extreme emotionalism of Marianne and her mother.

Chapter 2

John Dashwood expresses his intention of fulfilling the promise made to his dying father by providing an income for his half sisters. His wife, however, easily persuades him that he owes them nothing.

Commentary

In one of the most brilliant comic scenes of the novel, the naked greed and egotism of John and Fanny Dashwood are revealed through their own self-deception. Logic is perverted as the couple argue away the girls' right to any part of their father's large fortune, invoking sentiment (the claims of little Harry) to suit their coldly selfish purposes. Jane Austen's style is characterised by irony. We can see this in operation here through the Dashwoods' abuse of rational language which vainly strives to conceal the real motivation behind it. From the very beginning of the novel then, Jane Austen has established a moral environment for her characters, and this sets the tone for what is to follow.

Chapter 3

During the next six months, Mrs Dashwood watches with approval the growing friendship between Elinor and Edward Ferrars, Fanny Dashwood's brother. Marianne on the other hand, feels that a man so unassuming as Edward can never fulfil the role of passionate romantic lover.

Commentary

The love theme is introduced and with it another dominant concern of the novel, the interplay between personal and social experience. The moral framework of the book is strengthened as the Ferrars family come under attack. Edward's preference for the quiet domestic life marks him as a failure in their eyes. An interesting comparison is drawn between the Ferrars' and Marianne's attitudes to Edward. Marianne also judges him according to a superficial set of standards, although her criteria are those of artistic sensibility, not wordly success. This drawing of unexpected parallels is a hallmark of Austen's technique in this novel. As well as establishing contrasts between her characters and situations, she is careful to point out the dangers of over-simple moral categorisation.

Chapter 4

The discussion of Edward continues. Marianne speaks out her reservations about him to Elinor and questions her sister about her feelings. More reticent, Elinor is reluctant to commit herself to any declaration whilst the exact nature of the relationship between herself and Edward is still unresolved. Her evident vacillation is noticed by the whole family, and life at Norland becomes increasingly uncomfortable. When Mrs Dashwood receives the offer of a cottage at Barton Park, an estate belonging to a relative of hers, they are grateful for the opportunity to leave Norland behind.

Commentary

We are shown here Marianne's youthfulness in contrast to Elinor's greater maturity. Marianne's opinions are based on books she has read, not on any experience of life. Elinor's attempt to disabuse Marianne is guarded but considered, and suggests that she is trying to conceal her own uncertainties by rationalising Edward's behaviour. But Jane Austen is also deliberately keeping us as readers in the dark. Without the full information about Edward at our disposal, we too can only judge him on appearance. Can you see how future narrative developments are being prepared for here? Right from the beginning, Jane Austen keeps a tight control over the structuring of her plot, and every detail counts. Hints, for example, that we have been given about the inflexible attitude of the Ferrars family are reinforced at this point to be taken up again later on.

Chapter 5

Mrs Dashwood's preparations for moving are well under way, her tendency to extravagance being curbed by Elinor's prudent management. John Dashwood's final chance of performing his father's wishes in helping his stepmother and sisters slips away. Sadly, the women leave their home, Marianne's farewell being particularly prolonged.

Commentary

Jane Austen's realist vision dominates this chapter as she shows that economics are a determining factor in the women's situation. Mrs Dashwood, a sketchily drawn character, becomes slightly fuller here and we can see how she is to be developed as an older version of Marianne. Austen wants too to satirise the over-fanciful literature of her time. Marianne's farewell to Norland is a clever parody of contemporary literary excesses: the rhetorical questions, the love of nature and the apotheosis of place were all features found in popular romantic novels of the day.

Chapter 6

The move to Barton cottage is accomplished and the family's furniture is arranged comfortably. Their landlord, Sir John Middleton, and his wife, the grand relatives who live in Barton Park, call and invite the Dashwoods to dinner.

Commentary

In the description of Barton Cottage and its setting, Jane Austen continues to poke fun at certain literary conventions of her day, and especially at the current vogue for pastoral (the love of the countryside). The *sense and sensibility* theme is thus developed through the contrast between practical comfort and a picturesque appearance – Austen clearly comes down on the side of comfort – and this opposition is ironically paralleled in the figures of Sir John and Lady Middleton. The theme of manners gains emphasis: we can contrast the politeness and elegance of Lady Middleton's behaviour with the lack of warmth that lies beneath. In thinking about Austen's technique, note how even in a brief chapter such as this, she is able to employ a range of possible points of comparison, a central structural device of this novel.

Chapter 7

The Dashwoods spend an evening at Barton Park in the company of the Middletons, Lady Middleton's mother, Mrs Jennings, and a rather grave bachelor of thirty-five, Colonel Brandon. The characters are briefly described and elaborated as they respond variously to Marianne's performance on the piano.

Commentary
In this book, appearances are constantly deceptive, and we must be wary of making snap judgements. Mrs Jennings' loud vulgarity and Colonel Brandon's reserve are sufficient excuse for Marianne to dismiss them as unworthy of attention. But her assessment is later proved to be based on superficialities.

Characteristically, Jane Austen uses a trivial social occasion to transmit important moral messages. Here, amidst the idle chatter, she reveals certain fundamental criteria for judgement, as the real sensitivity and genuine feeling of the Dashwoods stands out against the shallowness of the Middletons.

Chapter 8
Mrs Jennings tries to matchmake between Colonel Brandon and Marianne. Her efforts are treated with contempt by Marianne who views Brandon as an elderly, infirm ascetic, her exact opposite in fact. In conversation with her mother she expresses her concern about Edward Ferrars and Elinor, whose mutual silence seems to her quite incompatible with the romantic feeling she imagines exists between them.

Commentary
Both the social and personal aspects of marriage are made the focus of attention here. Can you see how Jane Austen exposes mistaken opinions on this subject? Mrs Jennings' thoughts on suitability (based on social criteria) are as extreme as Marianne's (based on her notions of passionate behaviour). Marianne's naivety in her willingness to categorise Brandon is made comic, but at the same time with hindsight we can see that Austen is creating an ironic narrative counterpoint, neatly anticipating later developments in the story.

Chapter 9
Out on a walk with her younger sister, Margaret, Marianne falls and twists her ankle. She is carried home by a passing stranger who charms the Dashwoods with his good looks and manners. Sir John tells them that this is John Willoughby, the heir to a nearby estate, Allenham, who is making his annual visit to the neighbourhood.

Commentary

The meeting of Willoughby and Marianne deliberately parodies the lovers' meetings of contemporary sentimental fiction, and as such it lives up to the perfect encounter of Marianne's imagination. As always, however, Jane Austen deflates any currents of romantic idealism that might be present: note how Marianne's effusions about the beauty of the countryside are interrupted by rain; her fall occurs because she runs too fast – indeed all her certainties are disproved by unforeseen occurrences. Just as her enthusiasm for literature determines her views on life, so she cannot discriminate between what is important and what is trivial – her interest in Willoughby is fired by superficial details, such as his elegant name. But Austen is never over-harsh in her criticism of Marianne. Her failings are seen as those of youth and inexperience, and her basic integrity is never questioned.

Chapter 10

The relationship between Marianne and Willoughby quickly becomes intimate. With delight they discover shared interests and their opinions appear to coincide on all matters, including their criticism of Colonel Brandon's withdrawn manner. Elinor observes all this with some concern.

Commentary

Jane Austen elaborates the *sense and sensibility* motif through a series of developing contrasts. Willoughby evokes differing responses from the sisters that indicate the values of Elinor's *sense* over Marianne's *sensibility*. Willoughby himself and Colonel Brandon form another variant on this, ironically, for a reversal is to take place in our assessment of which character embodies *sense* and which *sensibility*. Note how the attraction between Marianne and Willoughby is described in terms of externals of taste and behaviour. Look too at the role Elinor is required to adopt by Jane Austen, and how her laconic comments serve to undercut Marianne's enthusiasm.

Chapter 11

Marianne's attachment to Willoughby becomes more intense and the status of their relationship as unofficial lovers is publicly acknowledged in the busy social round of Barton. Lonely, Elinor spends much time with Colonel Brandon, whose interest in Marianne is apparent, and who confides to Elinor something of his anxieties for Marianne's innocence.

Commentary

The narrative has now begun to shape itself largely through Elinor's perception of events, and her observations have by this time become a reliable source of judgement for the reader. This is a book which seems to have two heroines, but can you see how the one to whom nothing happens is subtly being made into the focus of interest? Austen picks up the theme of private and public experience as the chapter places the close personal involvement of Marianne and Willoughby in a context of social interaction, where little escapes notice. An alternative perspective on individual experience is given through Elinor, who is shown as isolated in an environment that can offer her no stimulation. The literary cult of sensibility emphasised the value of solitude as an opportunity for self-analysis and romantic reflection. Elinor's loneliness and her reflections are, however, shown in a quite different light.

Chapter 12

Elinor hears of two incidents which convince her that Marianne and Willoughby are unofficially engaged: first that Willoughby offers Marianne the gift of a horse (an offer which Elinor persuades her sister to refuse); secondly that Marianne has given Willoughby a lock of her hair. One evening at Barton Park, Margaret's indiscreet comments about romantic attachments embarrass both Elinor and Marianne. An arrangement is made for the following day for the party to visit Whitwell, an estate belonging to a friend of Colonel Brandon's.

Commentary

In her analysis of codes of behaviour, Jane Austen makes it clear that Marianne, Willoughby and Margaret all transgress approved limits. But manners and morals are linked in very complex ways. Margaret's innocent social errors are different in form from the more serious indiscretions of Marianne, while the full extent of Willoughby's fault is yet to be shown. In reading this scene we have to understand something about the strict guidelines that young women had to follow in Jane Austen's day. To accept an expensive gift from a man was only permissible if he was a near relation. Jane Austen later shows us the reasoning behind this. Marianne's belief that personal feeling should be the only guide in relationships is shown to be misplaced, as all her actions have reverberations in the enclosed society that surrounds and watches her with Willoughby: they cannot live in isolation. Both incidents then illuminate aspects of this major concern of the text: the integration of personal emotion into a world of public commitment.

Chapter 13

To the dismay of the assembled company, the visit to Whitwell is peremptorily cancelled as Colonel Brandon is called away suddenly to London. During the morning, Willoughby takes Marianne to visit Allenham, the estate he is due to inherit from a distant relative. Elinor tries to convince Marianne of the gross impropriety of visiting Allenham while its owner, Mrs Smith, is in residence.

Commentary

This book contains many unexpected occurrences, and Brandon's departure is one of the more dramatic of these. Can you see how it fits into another narrative scheme that Austen is building up? Partly too this episode tells us more about the nature of Barton society. Brandon's unavoidable departure becomes a subject for malicious gossip, the same sort of gossip which is at work on Marianne's avoidable tour of Allenham. Marianne's spontaneity emerges from all this as a quality which must be modified, for by ignoring the social codes, she is preparing the way for social and personal disaster. Brandon's insistence on secrecy on a matter of personal importance contrasts sharply with the demonstrative nature of Marianne's love affair with Willoughby.

Chapter 14

Mrs Jennings continues to speculate openly about Colonel Brandon's departure, while Elinor speculates silently about the status of Marianne's relationship with Willoughby. Mrs Dashwood mentions her plans for alterations to Barton Cottage, plans that Willoughby good-humouredly deplores.

Commentary
The feelings of uncertainty described in the first half of the chapter
are dramatised in the second half. Willoughby's comments on the
cottage are the first direct example we have of his charm and
affectionate manner – but his speeches are covert and full of
undeclared meaning, hints that are insufficient guarantee of
intention. His openness of manner is in fact deceptive and should
be compared with the meanings behind Brandon's silence. Mrs
Dashwood's plans for the cottage will never materialise: this is a
fine example of Austen's economical use of detail, providing a
fullness of texture to the pattern of plans and accidents that give
structure to the story.

Chapter 15
The next morning, Willoughby announces that he must leave for
London that day at the express wish of Mrs Smith, and that he
does not know when he will return. Marianne is prostrate with
grief, and Elinor and Mrs Dashwood are puzzled at the sudden-
ness of the news and at the formal manner of his leave-taking.
Elinor and her mother discuss the implications of Willoughby's
conduct.

Commentary
The parallels with Brandon's departure in Chapter 13 are obvious,
and we should bear in mind Willoughby's censorious attitude on
that occasion. Jane Austen is building patterns into her text that
invite questions from the reader. Once more, evidence is offered
for analysis without the full facts being given. How are we
supposed to read Willoughby's conduct? Note that Elinor and Mrs
Dashwood give us different possible interpretations. Part of the
enquiry into *sense* and *sensibility* concerns degrees of restraint.
The discussion of secrecy and openness relates directly to this, as
does the description of Marianne's uncontrolled display of grief.
Compare too Willoughby's speech here with his style of speaking
in the preceding chapter.

Chapter 16
Marianne's melancholy at Willoughby's absence dominates her
behaviour and affects the atmosphere of the household. Edward

Ferrars arrives unexpectedly to visit the Dashwoods, but his manner seems oddly distant.

Commentary

Through Marianne, Jane Austen continues to expose the self-indulgent aspects of *sensibility*. Note that Marianne cultivates misery by isolating herself from family activities, and that Mrs Dashwood's sympathy encourages her in this attitude. Marianne's excesses are treated comically, however, as well as critically. She cannot identify her lover accurately and mistakes Edward's figure for Willoughby. Edward's re-entrance into the story complicates matters. Why do you think Jane Austen brings him back at this point? Partly her reason is a formal one. He helps the patterns to develop: he functions as a foil to both Willoughby and Marianne by being so unlike them; he balances Brandon by being a lover with a secret; and he helps to move the focus of romantic interest from Marianne to Elinor.

Chapter 17

The warmth of Mrs Dashwood's welcome dispels Edward's cold-ness of manner, and the former family intimacy is almost fully regained. That evening their conversation together ranges from how they would each dispose of a fortune to their analysis of their own and each other's personalities.

Commentary

This brief chapter illuminates certain contrasts between fantasy and reality. The fixed opinions of Marianne on life and on love are in line with her failure to understand economic realities: both are based on romantic illusion and inexperience – she has been read-ing too many books! By contrast we can see the maturity of Elinor's insight in a crucial speech she makes about character. Read this particularly carefully, 'My doctrine has never aimed at the subjection of the understanding,' she tells Marianne. 'All I have ever attempted to influence has been the behaviour.' Dis-tinguishing between outward conformism and independence of thought, Elinor is acting partly as a projection of the author's voice. We need to recognise how Austen manipulates our reac-tions to Elinor. In this episode her view is the one upheld by the ultimate vision of the book.

Chapter 18

Elinor is disturbed by Edward's obvious low spirits. Further, Marianne embarrasses him by commenting on a ring containing a plait of hair that he is wearing. Edward says that the hair is his sister's but the girls believe it to be Elinor's.

Commentary

One of Jane Austen's pervasive concerns is the relationship between feeling and language. Edward's silent unhappiness forms an implicit contrast with Marianne's earlier expressive grief, and contributes to this theme. The remarks on the picturesque (a popular theory about artistic merit) also illuminate this idea. More centrally, we can begin to see now how the narrative sequence itself is actually constructed out of misunderstandings and misinterpretations, often based on inaccurate readings of evidence. How much should Edward say about his situation? The ring and its significance demonstrate the complexities of this question when it is explained later in the book. Analogies with the lock of hair given to Willoughby are invited, and, when the truth is revealed, throw new light on the significance of romantic gesture.

Chapter 19

After a week, Edward reluctantly leaves Barton, his plans about his future still unresolved. Mrs Jennings' other daughter, Mrs Palmer, and her family come to stay at Barton Park. On a call at the cottage, Mrs Palmer's volubility contrasts with both Lady Middleton's cold politeness and Mr Palmer's brusque incivilities. The visit concludes with a pressing invitation to the Dashwood girls to dine at the Park, an invitation they accept with great reluctance.

Commentary

The episode of Edward's visit demonstrates the subtlety with which Jane Austen presents issues, and shows how one small incident can furnish her with material for complex examination. For example, Elinor as well as Marianne is shown to be capable of error when she attributes Edward's behaviour to his mother's influence. We gain further insights into Edward's dependent situation. Ironically he is like Willoughby in his reliance on a woman's authority. We can also compare Elinor's reaction to his departure with Marianne's earlier behaviour. Austen makes us as readers work very hard. She directs our attentions to these comparisons in subtle ways. What she does stress is that Elinor's self-control should not be taken as an indication of shallow feelings. Elinor spends most of her time thinking about Edward, illustrating the disparity between independence of mind and outward conduct that she described to Marianne in Chapter 17. The arrival of the party from the Park provides a comic perspective on all this. Look at the ways in which the two sisters (Mrs Palmer and Lady Middleton) and Mr Palmer can be compared with the Dashwood girls and Edward, to the latter's clear moral advantage.

Chapter 20

During their evening at the Park, Elinor and Marianne try to resist Mrs Palmer's pressing attentions. Her husband's studied rudeness is in sharp contrast to her good-humoured gossip.

Commentary

It is typical of Jane Austen's ironic method that the most foolish characters should be agents of significant information. Mrs Palmer's aimless and silly chatter deals with matters of fundamental importance to the Dashwoods, and shows what can happen if forms of etiquette are ignored. She has spread news of Marianne's engagement to Willoughby: this is the result of the couple's rash behaviour. The chapter also contains some acid comments on the marriage market. Mr Palmer is an interesting forerunner of the cynical Mr Bennet in *Pride and Prejudice*. Can you see how Austen suggests the sorts of pressures that exist to persuade young women to marry? Her heroines Elinor and Marianne need this context to accentuate their personal stories.

Chapter 21

Distant cousins of Mrs Jennings, Anne and Lucy Steele, arrive for a visit at Barton Park. Sir John is effusive in their praise, but at their first meeting, Elinor assesses them as shallow and sycophantic. Anne Steele's conversation is particularly foolish and dominated by thoughts of beaux, but she arouses Elinor's curiosity by mentioning Edward Ferrars.

Commentary
The introduction of the Steele sisters offers yet another variant on the use of siblings in this novel. It is also a favourite Austen device to bring in an unpleasant character about halfway through who will influence the plot (Lady Catherine in *Pride and Prejudice* and Mrs Elton in *Emma* do the same job). The Steeles help us to measure the Dashwoods – not the moral suggestiveness of their name. However much we condemn Marianne, we can see her sterling qualities when we compare her with the Steeles. In Jane Austen's novels, characters often expose themselves through a careless use of language. Here the Steeles ape the jargon of sensibility, but lack sensitivity in its application. Their attitude towards love is mercenary and grasping. The Steeles in fact give us a new angle on what *sense* and *sensibility* can mean. Watch the way in which Austen uses the Middleton children here. It is just a brief incident, but it helps pursue the ideas about upbringing and character formation which are inherent in the portrayal of Marianne. It also deflates another tendency of sensibility, which was to idolise childhood innocence.

Chapter 22
Because Marianne ignores the Steeles, their company is forced on Elinor. One day, when they are walking alone together, Lucy Steele tells Elinor that she met Edward Ferrars when he was a pupil at her uncle's tutorial establishment, and that for the past four years she and Edward have been secretly engaged. Although much of the time, Jane Austen shows us the differences between Elinor and Marianne, she also stresses their similarity. Here, their judgement of the Steele sisters is identical, although they behave differently towards them.

Commentary
Edward is a character who appears little in the action, but who is constantly kept before the reader, either in reported accounts or in Elinor's thoughts. The management of this episode parodies a favourite situation of popular romantic novels of the time, containing as it does an engagement made in secret because of the opposition of a cruel parent, and told to a best friend in confidence. All these motifs are however used by Jane Austen to

reverse the reader's expectations. Lucy's announcement is deliberately calculated to hurt Elinor for instance. The scene shows
Elinor's restraint enduring its greatest test to date. The neatness of
textual patterning is evident in this section. Look for example at
how both Elinor and Lucy exert control over their feelings. Their
display of *sense* has different implications in each case.

Chapter 23
Alone, Elinor reflects on Lucy's news. She comes to the conclusion that Edward has become irrevocably trapped as a result of his
youthful infatuation. She also realises that her own sorrow must be
kept hidden from her family, whose sympathy for her and outright
condemnation of Edward would only distress her further. She
decides to seek another tête-à-tête with Lucy in order to clarify the
situation more precisely.

Commentary
The bulk of this chapter identifies us closely with Elinor's consciousness. The language, with its questions, exclamations and
attempts to rationalise closely follows the processes of her mental
workings – it is done with great subtlety, and is a technique we
associate normally with novels of a much later date. This dramatic
approach is interspersed with comments from the author and the
effect of Elinor's internal struggle is convincingly produced. One
result of this method is to sharpen the sense of Elinor's isolation
and if we contrast her behaviour here with Marianne's earlier
reaction to Willoughby, we get two views of *sensibility*, the
experience of feeling. The chapter ends with a description of the
boredom of Lady Middleton's drawing room. This is not just a
social detail, but places Elinor's inner life within a fully realised
environment, relating directly to a main theme of the book. Jane
Austen suggests that such absorption in their emotional lives is
perhaps inevitable given the restricted nature of the circle in which
the girls move.

Chapter 24
Elinor and Lucy have another lengthy conversation, after which
Elinor is convinced that the engagement between Lucy and
Edward is loveless. Lucy, having first made sure that the Dash-
woods have no plans to leave Barton, tells Elinor that she will
meet Edward in London during the winter season.

Commentaruy

This episode again demonstrates the subtlety of Jane Austen's methods and her brilliance in dialogue. How do we know that Lucy does not mean what she says? On the surface, the language is rational, polite and restrained. Underneath, the mutual dislike and jealousy of the two women is confirmed. Austen makes great use of innuendo and the potential double meanings of words and phrases. For instance, Lucy implies that Edward has given himself away by talking too much of Elinor, and that she knows full well the state of affairs between them. Note especially the play on the word 'indifferent'. Her malice and callousness dominate the conversation. This scene has further ironic implications. If we look carefully we can see that all Lucy's prophecies about Mrs Ferrars and the disinheritance ultimately come true.

Chapter 25

Mrs Jennings invites Elinor and Marianne to go with her to London for the winter. Elinor, however, needs to be persuaded by her mother and Marianne before she eventually accepts.

Commentary

In most of her novels, Jane Austen likes to move her characters from one environment to another as part of her examination of relationships between individuals and their communities. What do you think this achieves here? Bear in mind Jane Austen's interest in self-knowledge. The move to London initiates a fresh stage in Marianne's education. Their respective attitudes to Mrs Jennings' invitation indicate the sisters' different personalities. Elinor is cautious; she wishes to avoid situations where she knows she might be hurt, and finds the prospect of seeing Edward (and Lucy) painful. Marianne on the other hand cannot anticipate danger: she dismisses all problems in the light of her enthusiasm for seeing Willoughby again. Note Austen's tone of mockery at the emotional farewells of Marianne and her mother, yet one more in the series of leave-takings we find in this novel. An underlying theme of the book is the constancy of affection, as we are shown relationships that continue to flourish despite absence. Saying 'goodbye' too is seen as part of the natural pattern of experience, a pattern of order and interruptions.

Chapter 26

The sisters arrive at Mrs Jennings' London home after a three-day journey. Marianne writes at once to Willoughby and then spends her time in constant expectation of seeing him. Absorbed in thoughts of Willoughby, she can concentrate on nothing else, and the burden of social politeness falls on Elinor, who has to help entertain Mrs Jennings' callers, including Colonel Brandon.

Commentary
An ironic twist has been given to the sisters' assertions of the previous chapter. Elinor who wanted to stay quietly at home, finds herself forced into social activity. Marianne's eagerness for London life manifests itself as a withdrawal into her private reveries. Jane Austen is interested in ideas of social duty. The theme of manners is developed with Marianne's rudeness being met by Mrs Jennings' kindness, which ironically reverses our expectations of how characters behave. Look at how the contrast between Colonel Brandon and Charlotte Palmer is used as back-up material for this idea, and how the motifs of silence and volubility are reintroduced.

Chapter 27

Marianne is still obsessed by thoughts of Willoughby but she is not prepared to confide in Elinor. Her misery is increased when, at a small party at the Middletons', she learns that Willoughby too was asked but refused the invitation. Colonel Brandon asks Elinor what truth there is in the rumour that Willoughby and Marianne are engaged, and is clearly disturbed when she tells him that although she does not know the details, she is sure of their mutual affection.

Commentary
In reading the novel we need to be aware of the way in which Jane Austen handles the point of view from which we observe characters. Almost invariably we see Marianne's feelings only through Elinor's perception of them. The narrative method encourages us to identify with Elinor so that it comes as a shock here when Marianne accuses her of reserve (a term that implies coldness, insensitivity and indifference). The chapter clearly evokes the sense of tensions being present beneath the surface, partly through

Marianne's responses, but also through the evident strain in the sisters' relationship and through noting Brandon's struggle to control his feelings at the end. In order to appreciate the nuances of feeling, we have to understand something about the strictness of prevailing social codes. The fact that Marianne writes to Willoughby is taken by everyone as firm evidence that the couple are engaged. Ironically, Austen exploits one of the central features of the literature of sensibility, the significance attached to trivial detail, to establish the harsh nature of the real social world.

Chapter 28
At a large party, Marianne sees Willoughby in conversation with a young lady. Reluctantly he is forced to acknowledge her, but his manner is cold and formal. Marianne becomes distressed and has to leave.

Commentary
Jane Austen's observation of behavioural codes is brought to a climax here as Marianne's affectionate spontaneity is confronted by Willoughby's icy formality. Austen has moved her heroines from the fairly sheltered world of Barton into the harsher environment of London. Away from their mother's sympathy, they are more exposed to the unpleasantness of life. How severely do you think Austen judges her society here? We see how Marianne's belief in the genuineness of personal values is destroyed by Willoughby's terseness. He uses the language of stilted politeness to hide behind. We should compare Marianne's response here with Elinor's earlier resilience in the scene with Lucy Steele.

Chapter 29
Early in the morning, Marianne writes to Willoughby. She receives in return a brief note returning her gifts and letters and announcing his impending engagement to another woman. Marianne is distraught and Elinor is angry. Marianne tells Elinor that although her relationship with Willoughby was full of expressions of affection, there was never any explicit engagement between them.

Commentary

With this twist in the plot, the two sisters have now been placed in almost identical situations: each has lost the man she loves to a rival who cares nothing for him. Look at the stress placed on the contractual aspects of marriage. Marianne and Elinor's relationships, based on feeling, are nullified by a society which relies on legalities. Willoughby (who seemed the representative of sensibility) is now seen to resemble Lucy (the representative of hard sense) in marrying for money. Once more (as for example in John Dashwood's evasion of his father's wishes), natural feeling is set side by side against contractual obligation. We should note too here the use that Jane Austen makes of letters. Compare Marianne's style of writing, free, direct and utterly without guile, with Willoughby's, full of clichés and expressions calculated to hurt Marianne.

Chapter 30

Mrs Jennings confirms that news of Willoughby's engagement is widespread, and that his fiancée is Miss Grey, an heiress with fifty thousand pounds. At dinner, she treats Marianne with kindly consideration, and after Marianne has left the room she assures Elinor of her sympathy for her plight. She remarks that Willoughby's defection now leaves room for Colonel Brandon, and Brandon himself visits the house that evening, concerned about what he has heard.

Commentary

How do we view Mrs Jennings after reading this chapter? Although her attentions are misplaced and Marianne dismisses her as insensitive, we cannot mistake her goodheartedness. Her vulgarity does not negate her capacity for true feeling, and, ironically, it is this imperceptive and undiscriminating character who is allowed to prophesy Marianne's future. Jane Austen is adept at giving us little surprises throughout this novel both in terms of plot developments and the structure of ideas. We are continually being asked to re-assess characters and situations. Here, for example we are again offered that most unlikely parallel between two characters who seem to be exact opposites, Mrs Jennings and Marianne. Mrs Jennings' comments on Brandon's grave demeanour (she expects him to be overjoyed at the news about Willoughby) reveal her lack of insight. She is like Marianne in being too ready to judge on externals, and the comedy of her portrayal prevents us from taking Marianne's suffering too seriously.

Chapter 31

Marianne receives a letter from her mother innocently encouraging her hopes of Willoughby. In Mrs Jennings' absence, Colonel Brandon calls at the house and tells Elinor the story of his own tragic love affair. He explains that he had left Barton in order to find his sixteen-year-old ward, Eliza Williams, whom he discovered seduced and abandoned, having been betrayed by Willoughby. In conclusion, he admits that he has recently fought a duel with Willoughby over the brutal treatment of Eliza Williams.

Commentary

Colonel Brandon's story is told in a way that owes much to the popular tradition of eighteenth-century tales. Note how the style of this episode is at odds with the general ironic tone that governs most of the book. It is important to note too that Eliza's experience is given us second-hand, so that it does not interfere with the sense of comic decorum that the novel sustains. Brandon's story performs a variety of functions. First, his disclosures show how unfair are Marianne's casual assumptions about him and about the reasons for his visit: he too is capable of sincere feeling and this is the only occasion when the emotions that lie behind his normal reticence are presented to us directly. Secondly, Brandon gives us a view of Willoughby that we have not had before and the extent of his deception is exposed. Thirdly, and perhaps thematically most important, we are shown the realities that lie behind romantic idealism. The harsh details of Eliza's fate give us a picture of the massive penalties that are to be paid for ignoring social codes. Youth, innocence and poverty are all liabilities that should make women doubly careful in a world where they are reliant on male protection. Implicitly, this message relates directly to Marianne's situation, and suggests what might have been her fate too.

Chapter 32

Marianne's misery on hearing of Willoughby's villainy seems to change her personality. To her dismay, Mrs Dashwood advises the

girls to extend their stay in London, thinking this will be an
antidote to Marianne's depression. Elinor does what she can to
spare her sister from the pain of hearing gossip but has to deal with
the responses of Mrs Jennings' family and friends to the news
about Willoughby. Willoughby's marriage takes place. As he and
his bride leave London for the country, the Steele sisters arrive for
their planned visit.

Commentary
Marianne's dependent situation is stressed in her submission to her
mother's ruling. Look at how the patterns of sense and sensibility
are extended with even the minor characters such as the Middletons and the Palmers giving us variants on these concepts. Their
presentation goes beyond providing comic relief: it creates a wider
perspective for us to view Marianne's grief. In this way Austen
manages to convince us of the immediate impact of her misery,
while simultaneously reassuring us that in time she will recover.
The action continually switches our interest from one sister to
another. Here, the Steeles' arrival, timed neatly to coincide with
Willoughby's departure, serves to remind us of Elinor's continued
but silent state of suffering.

Chapter 33
Marianne and Elinor accompany Mrs Jennings on some errands.
At a jeweller's shop, Elinor's attention is caught by a young man
choosing a toothpick case. At the same shop they meet their
brother, John, who apologises for not having called on his sisters,
explaining that he and Fanny have only recently arrived in
London. The next day he visits them and tells Elinor of Edward's
forthcoming marriage to an heiress, Miss Morton. He complains of
his own penury and remarks on his sisters' marriage prospects,
suspecting an alliance between Elinor and Colonel Brandon.

Commentary
The satiric tone of this chapter moves from observation of
extravagance and misplaced attention to detail (the fastidious
choice of a toothpick case) to a sustained dramatic exhibition of
meanness and materialism in John Dashwood's speeches. The
news about Edward's marriage plans gives a new twist to the plot.
We have here yet another example of important information

conveyed by a silly character. It also suggests further ironic parallels between characters who seem most dissimilar: Elinor, Marianne and Lucy Steele all now seem to share the position of having been rejected by their lovers.

Chapter 34

Mr and Mrs John Dashwood give a dinner party at which Mrs Ferrars is to be present. Elinor worries beforehand that she might meet Edward there, having received his visiting card as proof that he is in London. The Steele sisters also procure an invitation and at the party they receive flattering attentions from Mrs Ferrars and Fanny Dashwood, who are both determined to slight Elinor for what they believe to be her designs on Edward.

Commentary
This chapter contains numerous ironies of detail that add to the narrative and thematic patterns of the text. Elinor's anxiety about the party resembles Marianne's attitude to the earlier Middleton party; Edward, like Willoughby on that occasion, is deliberately absent. Note how the parallelism extends to minutiae; the *two* calling cards left when the sisters are out. The episode cleverly exploits the discrepancies in levels of knowledge between Mrs Ferrars, Lucy and Elinor in the battle for Edward. The chapter also asks us to question accepted views on what constitutes good manners. For example, Mrs Ferrars' and her daughter's insistence on elegance and etiquette emerges as rudeness, while Marianne's rudeness over the firescreen incident is perceived as loyalty and courage. We are reminded of the importance of good sense and again the centrality of Mrs Jennings' position can be seen. Her vulgarity does not inhibit her right thinking (she sums up Fanny and later Mrs Ferrars accurately), nor her loyalty and goodheartedness in her support for Marianne.

Chapter 35

The following morning, Lucy visits Elinor in order to gloat over her supposed success of the previous day with Mrs Ferrars. While they are talking, Edward arrives unexpectedly, to the extreme embarrassment of all three. Elinor manages to recover social composure, but when Marianne enters and greets Edward with open affection, the situation becomes strained and the visit is soon

over. Bound by her vow of secrecy, Elinor cannot explain to
Marianne the real facts of the situation.

Commentary

We need to be particularly alert here to the way in which Jane
Austen produces her comic effects. Once more the source of the
irony relies on the reader's understanding of the different levels of
knowledge that exist between the characters. Because of our
superior knowledge, we can see that what Lucy intends as cruelty
loses its force because she doesn't know about Miss Morton. The
moral dimension is as strong as ever and we can see clearly how
malicious she is in her attempts to crush Elinor, and in her pointed
comments to Marianne about broken engagements. Watch how
Jane Austen delicately balances the Dashwood sisters' behaviour.
Here, when Elinor is in danger of declining, Marianne's vitality
gains ascendance. Previously the reverse was the case. The
discussion about broken promises takes on deeper meaning, and is
concluded by Elinor's fidelity to her promise to Lucy, ironically
the character to whom she owes least.

Chapter 36

Mrs Jennings goes each day to visit her daughter Charlotte who
has just had a baby. Consequently, Elinor and Marianne spend
their days at the Middletons in the company of the Steeles, much
to their mutual dislike. At an evening party, Elinor meets Edward's brother, Robert Ferrars, whom she recognises as the young
man she had noticed in the jeweller's. John Dashwood suggests to
his wife that they should invite his sisters to stay with them. In
order to avoid this, Fanny immediately asks the Steeles instead.
Ignorant of the circumstances that have prompted the invitation,
Lucy construes it as a mark of particular favour.

Commentary

With the introduction of Robert Ferrars, the family patterns of the
novel are complete. The chapter deals with family relationships,
from Mrs Jennings' concern for her daughter to Fanny's rejection
of her husband's sisters, via Lady Middleton's obsession with her
children. A range of examples are offered on the theme of natural
feeling and family duty. The attack on affectation which we find
throughout the novel, culminates here with Robert Ferrars. His

speech about cottages echoes the extremist language of sensibility (remember what we have said about the idealisation of the pastoral), while clearly demonstrating his own conceit and materialism.

Chapter 37

Mrs Jennings tells Elinor that Anne Steele, misinterpreting the feelings of the Ferrars family, has informed Fanny Dashwood about the engagement between Lucy and Edward. In the resulting uproar, Fanny has turned the Steeles out of the house. Elinor is now compelled to explain the situation to Marianne, who is full of remorse at having previously thought her sister unfeeling. John Dashwood visits his sisters to give his version of events, and to tell them that Mrs Ferrars has disinherited Edward in favour of his younger brother, Robert.

Commentary

The disclosures of this chapter serve a variety of purposes. Look first at how complex Elinor's response is – she must try to retain the mask of impartiality in public and must undeceive Marianne in private. Her explanation to Marianne provides a rational analysis of subtle family and social obligations that surround and constrain the expression of personal feeling.

This works as a positive force on Marianne's own growth in understanding. However, the seriousness of this passage is framed by two comic scenes, each of which highlights the distinction between false and genuine interpretations. Mrs Jennings with only partial knowledge sees what has happened as a romantic interlude, just like those in popular literature (again, note the parallel with Marianne) where young lovers are forbidden to marry by a snobbish parent. The visit of John Dashwood balances this and moves the scene into high comedy. His speech is a brilliant piece of burlesque. He defends egoism, snobbery, obstinacy, callousness and materialism in terms that travesty the language of sensibility. Ironically, Edward, the man whom Marianne believed to be the antithesis of a romantic lover, now has to act out that part to perfection. The irony is deepened by the fact that his behaviour is based on a code of honour that he upholds despite the fact that he no longer loves Lucy.

Chapter 38

Out walking, Elinor meets Anne Steele who informs her that Edward and Lucy's engagement will continue, although Edward offered Lucy the chance to break it now that he has been disinherited. The following day, Elinor receives a letter from Lucy which gives an alternative version of events, describing Edward's determination to keep to the engagement despite her attempts to persuade him to end it. She tells Elinor that the only thing that stands in the way of their marriage is Edward's lack of income.

Commentary

Continually in this novel we find that truth is obscured and is filtered to us through unreliable narrators, here Anne and Lucy Steele. Elinor must sift what she has been told to get at the facts. Her sense of justice and honour are paramount: look how her attitude changes when she realises that Anne's information has been gained by underhand means (listening behind doors). Read Lucy's letter especially carefully. It is a masterpiece of dual meanings and produces its intended effects on both Mrs Jennings and Elinor independently.

Chapter 39

Elinor and Marianne agree to accompany Mrs Jennings to the Palmers' house at Cleveland in Somerset *en route* for home. Marianne is nervous about being in the same county as Willoughby. Colonel Brandon having heard the news about Edward and Lucy wants to offer Edward the living on his estate, Delaford, which has just become vacant. Apologetic about the limited income it provides, he asks Elinor to inform Edward of his offer.

Commentary

Once again we are faced with oblique messages. The conversation between Elinor and Brandon is overheard by Mrs Jennings, who comically misinterprets it, attributing Elinor's obvious emotion to a proposal of marriage. The theme of illusion and imperfect knowledge is continued through Brandon here. Even the most valued character, Jane Austen reminds us, is capable of error. His generosity in this instance is quite misplaced, unwittingly making Elinor the agent of her lover's marriage to another woman. When

Austen refers to a 'living', she means the position of vicar to the locality of the estate, a job which was often in the gift of the estate owner.

Chapter 40
Mrs Jennings congratulates Elinor on what she believes to be her engagement to Brandon, and a conversation ensues full of misunderstandings, which are only clarified at the end of the chapter. While Elinor is trying to compose a letter to Edward to inform him of Brandon's offer, Edward himself arrives and she is able to tell him about it in person. Both realise with dismay that there are now no obstacles in the way of his marriage to Lucy.

Commentary
Jane Austen uses different types of comedy in this book. Here, the situation between Elinor and Mrs Jennings borders on farce. Remember that Mrs Jennings, so eager to congratulate Elinor, has always assumed that Brandon was in love with Marianne. The scene between Elinor and Edward offsets this. Instead of mutual verbal confusion, it is full of mutual but unspoken understanding, the exact antithesis of what had gone before.

Chapter 41
Lucy is vociferous in her gratitude to Elinor for facilitating her marriage. Elinor visits her brother and discovers that the Ferrars family resent Brandon's generosity to Edward. John cannot believe that the gift could be made without ulterior motive. Elinor's dislike of Robert Ferrars, who is also present, is consolidated. His manner towards Edward is casual and mocking. Having accepted the inheritance, he is prepared to profit by it and abandon Edward to relative poverty. In addition, he makes insulting remarks about Lucy.

Commentary
The episode at the Dashwoods' reinforces the moral dimension of the text by contrasting the selfishness, deceit and malice of John, Fanny, Mrs Ferrars and Robert with Elinor's integrity and natural sense of right. Gradually, our perceptions of Elinor are being altered. She is no longer a passive observer in this scene, but her intelligence is actively at work in her quick analysis of situation

and personality (she sums up Robert Ferrars immediately). Jane Austen's comic vision always involves an admiration of wit, and Elinor's asperity here is in sharp contrast to her earlier manner of resigned politeness. Her sarcasm is however lost on John and Robert, their stupidity neatly illuminating her perspicacity.

Chapter 42
Elinor and Marianne leave London and arrive at Cleveland, where they find themselves surprisingly comfortable with the Palmers. Colonel Brandon is also a visitor and, despite Mrs Jennings, Elinor still believes him to be secretly in love with Marianne. Marianne's thoughts return to Willoughby and, seeking solitude, she spends her time wandering alone through the grounds of Cleveland, as a result of which she catches a severe cold.

Commentary
Sense and *sensibility* are once more the dominant motifs of this chapter. The busy sociability of the Palmers' way of life contrasts with the self-imposed solitude of Marianne. If we accept that *sense* and *sensibility* equate to some extent with public and personal levels of experience, we can see how Austen formulates her enquiry, relating conceptual issues to realistic conditions. Austen's insistence on practical detail deflates any sentimental attitudes. The picturesque landscape that Marianne finds so attractive was a favourite literary environment for reflecting on blighted love. In this novel, however, it consists of wet grass, which soaks Marianne's stockings and gives her a bad cold.

Chapter 43
Marianne's cold turns feverish, and the Palmers, concerned over danger of infection to their new baby, leave the house. Marianne's condition deteriorates and she becomes delirious. Fearing for her life, Elinor sends Colonel Brandon to fetch Mrs Dashwood to Cleveland. Watching at Marianne's bedside, Elinor sees the fever abate. Relieved she sits down to wait for her mother, but instead it is Willoughby who arrives at the house.

Commentary
This is a crucial chapter. The turning point of Marianne's fever is also a turning point for several of our attitudes as readers. For

instance, we must radically re-assess our position *vis-à-vis* Elinor and what she embodies. We have previously been encouraged to identify with her and admire her common sense, but this is now shown to be ineffective. Neither her stoicism nor her medical treatment can alter the progress of Marianne's illness. We also witness for the first time the breakdown of Elinor's composure, as her anxiety about Marianne is made the focus of the episode. The novel which has so far appeared to endorse the values of order now confronts us dramatically with the overwhelming power of chance, the unpredictable element in human experience. This has of course been prepared for all the way through the book: think of the reasons for all those surprises. Marianne's illness, its development, her sudden recovery, the fluctuations in Elinor's feelings and Willoughby's arrival are all outside Elinor's control and quite beyond the power of reasoning. At this late stage in the novel then we are offered a radically new perspective on ideas about sense and sensibility.

Chapter 44

Despite Elinor's initial reluctance to admit him, Willoughby insists on telling her his story. He describes how he unintentionally fell in love with Marianne and how he was on the point of proposing marriage to her when he was threatened with disinheritance by Mrs Smith, who had heard of the Eliza Williams affair. Deeply in debt, he saw in Miss Grey the solution to his financial problems. He was horrified to learn of Marianne and Elinor's presence in London, but his hand was forced by Miss Grey, who had dictated the letter of rejection to Marianne. Willoughby pleads for Elinor's forgiveness and departs, leaving her in turmoil.

Commentary

This episode continues the conceptual questioning started in the previous chapter. Willoughby's account offers a new look at events that Elinor thought she was sure about. Her response to Willoughby also reveals the complex factors that determine relationships, and the tensions that can exist between sympathy and judgement. Jane Austen constantly uses individual personalities and specific events to explore abstract issues, and here we find a penetrating enquiry into the nature of moral categories. With all his faults, Willoughby cannot be easily dismissed as a stock villain.

He will not fit into either of the conventional literary roles (romantic hero or vile seducer) that have previously been allotted him, for he is a more complex creation. Despite her standpoint of moral criticism for his actions, Elinor warms to Willoughby's charm, that elusive element in personality which cannot be quantified, and by so doing shows her own susceptibility to irrational feelings.

Chapter 45

Mrs Dashwood arrives at Cleveland. Her joy at Marianne's recovery is compounded by her delight in the fact that Colonel Brandon has declared to her his love for Marianne. Elinor listens to her mother's raptures with mixed feelings, pleased that she has encouraged Brandon, sceptical of her outright censure of Willoughby and disappointed that her own troubles seem to have been ignored.

Commentary

Jane Austen uses this chapter to enquire further into the meaning of *sensibility*. The profound quality of Elinor's emotion is thrown into relief by the extremism of Mrs Dashwood, whose spontaneity reminds us here of the early Marianne. The genuine nature of her feeling is commendable, but the quickness of her reactions (especially her speedy reversal of attitude to Brandon) seems shallow against the enduring strength of Elinor's emotions. Look at the way in which Mrs Dashwood's imagination goes to work. We gain an insight here into the cause of Marianne's early follies, given the nature of parental influence on character.

Chapter 46

Marianne is soon well enough to return home to Barton to complete the slow process of recovery. Out walking with Elinor, she begins to talk of Willoughby. She acknowledges her own past failings and determines on an improved policy for the future. Encouraged by her sister's calmness, Elinor tells her of the conversation she had with Willoughby at Cleveland.

Commentary

By this stage we can see that the two sisters are gradually changing roles. Hitherto unrevealed aspects of their personalities now

become dominant in their presentation. Elinor begins to approximate the traditional heroine of sensibility, as minute gradations
of feeling become significant in determining her life. The more
serious and thoughtful side to Marianne's nature takes over from
her initial uncurbed enthusiasm. Note especially Marianne's long
speech. Like other Jane Austen *ingénues*, she has acquired
self-knowledge through her painful experiences, *but* the comic
view is maintained. Her insistence on future virtue is a satiric jibe
on Jane Austen's part at another sort of literary stereotype, the
exemplary moral paragon and reformed character who was
another favourite figure found in the novels of the age.

Chapter 47

Elinor, Marianne and Mrs Dashwood discuss Willoughby's conduct. The others agree with Elinor that his earlier behaviour was
motivated by self-interest. Elinor is surprised to receive no news of
Edward. One day a servant tells them that Lucy Steele and Mr
Ferrars are now married. Observing her daughters' strong reac-
tions to the news, Mrs Dashwood realises that she has misjudged
the depth of Elinor's love for Edward.

Commentary

Again this is a most carefully patterned scene, as the interest
moves from Willoughby to Edward. For the first time, the irony is
directed to provide a comic view of Elinor. Immediately after her
speeches full of reasoned argument and moral precepts, she is
rendered speechless by her powerful emotion on hearing the news
of the marriage. As the novel moves towards its close we should
note Jane Austen's strict adherence to a sense of comic decorum.
She maintains a detachment from her characters. The ironic asides
about Margaret for instance prevent us from identifying too
closely with Elinor's sense of shock. Look at how under pressure,
the sisters revert to type. It is now Marianne who becomes
hysterical, Elinor who remains silent. Austen is again mocking the
popular novels of the period with the portrayal of Mrs Dashwood
in this scene. Contrary to normal practice, in Jane Austen's work it
is the mother who learns from her children, not vice versa.

Chapter 48

While Elinor is struggling to come to terms with the idea of
Edward's marriage, Edward himself arrives unannounced at Bar-

ton Cottage. After an awkward start, he tells the Dashwoods that it is his brother Robert who has married Lucy.

Commentary
This delightful episode contains several details that force comparisons with previous scenes of the novel. We can for instance compare Elinor's situation now with Marianne's after hearing of Willoughby's marriage; like Marianne, Elinor too mistakes the identity of her lover when he first arrives (but observe the way in which Austen plots the actual process of her feelings as she recognises Edward); again, like Marianne earlier, she is quite unable to control the expression of her emotion. Edward's arrival recalls Willoughby's sudden appearance at Cleveland. Our view of Edward is also altered by this scene. For the first time his behaviour is described directly, not through the filtering consciousness of Elinor. Look how Austen suggests the existence of unspoken but powerful emotion in Edward's mindless action with the scissors.

Chapter 49
Edward and Elinor become engaged. Edward explains the circumstances of his entanglement with Lucy and of his unexpected release. Thinking about their impending marriage, they realise that their income is too small to support them. Elinor urges Edward to go to London to seek his mother's assistance. Colonel Brandon accompanies him as far as Delaford.

Commentary
Can you see here how Austen controls the comic view of characters and events while still dealing with essentially serious matters? She allows ironic asides at the expense of both Elinor and Edward for instance, and the moments of greatest emotion (such as the proposal) take place off stage. Nothing is allowed to disturb the tone. In the process of clarification, comic misunderstandings still persist, and the humorous aspects (Mrs Jennings' letter, Brandon's delusions about Edward) are cleverly balanced against the more consequential (the revelations of Lucy's deceit, the complications with Mrs Ferrars). The subject of marriage now emerges as the central focus, the point towards which all events have been working, and in its accommodation of personal feelings

with economic realities it amalgamates the ideas of *sense* and *sensibility* which have been developed throughout.

Chapter 50
Mrs Ferrars gives Edward and Elinor ten thousand pounds on the occasion of their marriage, although she does not reinstate Edward's full rights of inheritance. Edward and Elinor marry and move to Delaford parsonage. Lucy, who has cunningly inveigled Robert into marriage, as cunningly ingratiates herself into Mrs Ferrars' favour. Marianne eventually realises the strength of Brandon's love for her and marries him, to the delight of her family and friends. Willoughby learns that had he behaved honourably to Marianne, Mrs Smith would have forgiven all.

Commentary
This chapter is concerned with resolution. In tying up all the loose ends, Jane Austen keeps her comic distance and gives us an authoritative overview of events. She is aware of what she is doing here as an author – we could say that she is making a point of the artificiality of the ending. The patterns of relationships between husbands/wives, mothers/children, sisters/brothers are emphatically reinforced to point up moral issues. The positive values of natural feeling are set against the negative qualities of callousness, injustice, greed and self-interest. The reversal of roles of the Dashwood sisters continues, as it is Elinor who marries for love, like the heroine of sensibility, and Marianne who makes the marriage of common sense, contradicting all her initial opinions on second attachments, middle-aged men and her thoughts about passion.

3 THEMES AND ISSUES

3.1 THE ANALYSIS OF FEELING

The analysis of feeling is a predominant concern in Jane Austen's novels, all of which show the progress of a young woman towards marriage based on love. In *Sense and Sensibility*, it is a central focus for Jane Austen's examination of the relationship between self and society. The enquiry into feeling is conducted on two main levels: first, the attempt to distinguish between genuine feeling and the false forms of emotional expression; secondly, to explore the way in which personal emotion, wayward and irrational in nature, can be contained within an ordered structure. Literary satire is Jane Austen's starting point for this exploration.

For *Sense and Sensibility* starts as an attack on the sentimental novels which abounded in the late eighteenth century, but it develops into something far more substantial in scope. Jane Austen was aware of the hysterical and extravagant behaviour that featured in much of the pulp fiction of her day, and many of the incidents in her own novel deliberately parody the conventional episodes of the literature of sensibility with which she was familiar. Initially this satire is directed through the portrayal of Marianne Dashwood, and when we start to read *Sense and Sensibility*, it seems as if she is going to be its central character. Marianne is a version of the sort of heroine to be found in these popular novels. Like them, she is young, exceptionally pretty, lives in a cottage with her widowed mother and, as the book opens, she is being cheated of a fortune. She is also at the centre of a range of melodramatic events – her passionate first love affair; her dramatic and public rejection;   the revelation of her lover's villainy;   her grave illness that brings her close to death; her eventual marriage to a wealthy husband – the synopsis reads like the well-tried plots of trite romance. But Jane Austen takes these motifs and manipulates them to form an investigation into what constitutes true sensibility and how influential it should be in determining a code of living.

In reading *Sense and Sensibility*, we must try to understand how the elements of literary burlesque are employed to serious purpose. Much of the conception of Marianne's character relies on noticing the ways in which she both resembles and differs from the traditional sentimental heroine. She tries to model her own life on a code of values lifted from the cult of sensibility. Her farewell to Norland, her playing the piano, her love of poetry, her country rambles: all have their source in a literary prototype that she admires, and she continually measures her own experiences against a set of literary ideals. Her disgust at Edward, for instance, in Chapter 3, stems from his failure to approximate the passionate heroes of her fictive imagination. Several incidents in the book are deliberate copies of those in popular novels and are used by Jane Austen to expose the deficiencies of sensibility as defined by that genre. Marianne's meeting with Willoughby, for example, perfectly recreates the conditions of a lovers' encounter of her fantasies, but the rapid development of their affair, instead of testifying to the instantaneous nature of love, shows rather its lack of solid foundation.

It has been suggested that Jane Austen is too harsh in her treatment of Marianne and that Marianne's story is intended to deflate the claims of romantic love and to mock at powerful feeling. I don't think that this is true at all. Although Marianne certainly changes from the wildly enthusiastic and passionate being shown at the outset of the novel to a much more tranquil character, Jane Austen never denies the intensity of Marianne's emotion, and we are meant to admire her genuine sensitivity and her capacity for strong feeling. Her grief, for example, at the loss of Willoughby, is surely heartfelt in comparison say with Lucy's pretence at sorrow on being parted from Edward. What Jane Austen criticises is Marianne's confusion as to what sensibility really means. Marianne thinks that the proof of feeling lies in its demonstrable effects. She refuses to look below the surface and therefore mistakenly dismisses Elinor as cold, failing to notice her misery because she does not see her weep nor look mournful.

By basing her life on a literary model, Marianne ironically denies the very quality of spontaneity she seeks to express. Without realising it, she is trying to follow a set of imposed rules for sentimental behaviour. She also creates a series of problems for herself, because life, Jane Austen insists, is very different from literature. Marianne's indulgence in melancholy after Willoughby's departure for London, exemplary behaviour for a heroine of sensibility, is shown in this novel to feed her own sense of unhappiness and to have adverse effects on those around her, especially Elinor. Similarly her insistence on solitude, another 'sentimental' feature, has social reverberations at Mrs Jennings' house, and more serious consequences at Cleveland where it nearly causes her death. Conventional sensibility, with its undue emphasis on self, is presented by Jane Austen as a form of egoism and is consequently invested with moral overtones. The censure of Marianne's self-absorption is modified by comparison with the selfishness of other characters in the novel, such as John and Fanny Dashwood, or Robert Ferrars, but Jane Austen does place Marianne's adherence to the forms of sensibility in a context that illuminates its defects.

In all her books Jane Austen argues against extremism, but we should not therefore conclude that she is necessarily anti-romantic. The portrayal of Elinor perfectly balances that of Marianne as Jane Austen explores through her the nature of silent and sustained love. Elinor's story demonstrates that good sense is not incompatible with sensibility. Elinor's restraint and her placidity of tone do not negate her susceptibility to sensation. 'Her mind was inevitably at liberty: her thoughts could not be chained elsewhere,' Jane Austen tells us. Without publicity, her thoughts and feelings are riotous 'in every possible variety which the different states of her spirits at different times could produce' (ch. 19). Elinor is the forerunner of other Austen portraits of quiet emotional constancy. Jane Bennet, Fanny Price, Jane Fairfax and Anne Elliot are all dominated by an unspoken love which is ever-present beneath their unruffled demeanour. Note that two of these are heroines of the novels in which they appear, while two are merely secondary characters. It is a favourite device of Jane

Austen's to provide us with pairs of young women who offer contrasting and mutually informing approaches to the subject of love.

Elinor is in love with Edward from the beginning of the novel, and although she would be for eighteenth-century readers an unusual choice for a heroine – she is not the prettiest of the three sisters, she does not attract universal admiration, she is not especially talented in her 'accomplishments' – she yet conforms ironically in several ways to the paragon of sensibility to be found in many of the conventional novels of the period. She is often lonely, she is self-analytical, she reflects frequently on her condition, she is constant to a seemingly faithless lover. More importantly, her feelings are as violent as Marianne's – do not forget how she almost faints when confronted by Lucy Steele's revelation. For Jane Austen, love is often transmuted into suffering. Yet Elinor tries to control, if not her actual emotion, then its public expression, and she avoids creating situations that are likely to exacerbate her own sense of sorrow. What we find therefore in the presentation of the two Dashwood sisters, is not that one embodies 'sense' and the other 'sensibility', but that they give us two alternative insights into what sensibility means.

Sentimentalists held quite categoric views about the way in which true feeling should operate. Marianne believes, for instance, in the power of first love which can never be supplanted. This notion is refuted in the novel both by Marianne's own experience and by Colonel Brandon's story. Their eventual marriage is one beteen partners each of whom has been in love before. It is ironically Elinor, whose love never wavers, who conforms to the ideal standard of sentimentalism. Continually we find that Jane Austen introduces literary parallels on the subject of feeling that deepen the analysis of the theme and our sense of the deceptive quality of appearances. Edward, for example, the reverse of the traditional lover of Marianne's dreams, reproduces conventionally 'heroic' behaviour in the affair with Lucy, when, disinherited by his family, he stands by the girl from a poor family to whom he is betrothed. And it is Brandon, the very antithesis of a dashing young gallant, who fights a duel to defend a lady's honour, an action straight out of the pages of fictional romance.

All the characters in *Sense and Sensibility* relate in some way to this question of feeling and are judged according to their potential for genuine response and love. So we find a pastiche of sentimental attitudes in the behaviour of the Steele sisters, whose protestations of affection and whose declared interest in 'beaux' and romance are exposed as grasping avarice. Those characters who most advertise their emotions are those whose motives are most suspect. It is, conversely, the most subdued affection which tends to be shown as the most enduring and the most profound, as in the cases of Elinor, Edward and Brandon. It is part of Jane Austen's ironic perspective that a novel which appears to be an attack on sentimentalism ends up by probing and endorsing feeling as a central moral principle in life.

Jane Austen's interest in forms of sensibility is not confined to romantic love, although this is her main focus. The presentation of families in the novel extends the theme to develop another angle on personal relationships. Those characters who are deficient in spontaneous family affection are severely condemned. Feeling might not always be responsibly managed, as is sometimes the case with Mrs Dashwood's misplaced sympathy for her daughters, but its existence is recognised as right and natural. Mrs Ferrars' callousness towards Edward, when her love is translated into monetary terms, is an extreme version of all that is most unnatural. Mrs Ferrars deviates in the most fundamental respect from the norm of human response in her rejection of Edward in favour of Robert, and particularly in her subsequent heartlessness towards his plight. These images of cruelty, or lack of feeling, recur in the novel in the distorted sets of relationships we see between parents and children, and beteen siblings. Think of Robert's gloating over Edward's misfortune in Chapter 41; or of Lucy's disloyalty to her sister in Chapter 22. The cold apathy of Lady Middleton is only one degree removed from this.

In *Sense and Sensibility* Jane Austen establishes a standard of natural feeling against which all characters are measured, and provides us with surprising instances of where true sensibility is to be found. Mrs Jennings, for instance, is a woman quite without finesse, who yet exhibits an instinctive charity, sympathy and unlimited affection that provide her with an unerring guide for action. She is Jane Austen's comic version of the heroine of sensibility, the antithesis of Marianne, with no consciousness of aesthetic refinement, but redeemed by her overwhelming good-heartedness. Marianne's over-hasty repudiation of Mrs Jennings is intended to serve as a warning against making snap judgements about the nature of the feeling heart, against confusing the subtleties of the sentimental poseur with an intrinsic capacity for love. In her warmth towards her family, her generosity to the Dashwoods and her universal goodwill, Mrs Jennings is placed high in the moral ranking order of the novel.

The analysis of feeling is one of Jane Austen's most pervasive and recurrent themes. In *Sense and Sensibility* she reacts initially against the artifical cultivation of an excess of sensibility with the satiric portraits of false feeling (Lucy Steele) or those who set themselves up as sophisticated connoisseurs (Robert Ferrars). She tries to restore the balance by identifying the constituents of genuine emotion as the opposite of showy by presenting the problems that confront a sensitive personality such as Elinor or Edward in a society, which as I shall go on to argue, is largely indifferent to personal values.

3.2 SOCIAL BEHAVIOUR

The world that Jane Austen chooses to show us in *Sense and Sensibility* is a world confined to a small segment of English middle-class society. As we read the novel we are made aware of a highly organised and stratified community where people are very conscious of precise class levels. At the top are the landed gentry, such as Sir John Middleton and Colonel Brandon who own large country estates. At the bottom are the Steele sisters, whose father keeps a small private school in a provincial town. In between we have a selection of characters whose position is determined by a subtle mix of factors relating to birth, wealth and breeding. The action of *Sense and Sensibility* moves between the country and the town – most of the characters who appear in one turn up in the other – and we are invited to compare rural and urban lifestyles. Through looking closely at this small segment, Jane Austen is making certain observations about the operation of society as a whole, and its effect on individual lives.

From the very beginning of the novel we are shown how movements within the rigid structure can take place. Sometimes these are beyond anyone's control. Mrs Dashwood finds that, with the death of her husband, her social position has shifted. From being the mistress in control of a large house and servants, she is now a dependent with no home of her own and with only a meagre income. Throughout the book we can see changes of this nature occur, often quite suddenly: the Ferrars' sons replace one another; Lucy Steele moves up several rungs of the social ladder with her marriage to Robert. Mrs Jennings, a rich widow from humble beginnings, is looked down upon by the snobbish Mrs Ferrars, but her daughters have managed to secure refined husbands through their wealth and beauty, and thus have acquired respectability one generation later. In charting these social developments, Jane Austen is at pains to point out that this sort of prestige carries with it no corresponding moral cachet. The moral order of the novel is quite distinct from the hierarchy of social class.

One of the dominant features of Jane Austen's novels is the social occasion, where the importance of observing the proprieties is stressed. Much of the action of *Sense and Sensibility* takes place at dinner-parties, dances, on morning calls and at other similar gatherings, where good manners are the arbiter of social acceptance or exclusion. Look at how the Steele sisters try to impress the Middletons and later the Ferrars with their superficial polish in order to gain entrance into the fashionable world. At these gatherings there is a code of rules to be observed, and deviation from these rules can be severely punished. The Steeles are evicted unceremoniously when Anne Steele presumes too far; Eliza Williams suffers a far worse fate. Sometimes the rules depicted seem to us to be strange and without rational foundation – why should Marianne not visit Allenham if she wants? The rigorous formalities that Jane Austen presents could almost be referring to a foreign culture that bears little relation to our own.

In order to understand these codes of manners, it is helpful to know that Jane Austen was writing with a well-established literary tradition in mind, the tradition of the conduct novel. One of the first of these was *Sir Charles Grandison* by Samuel Richardson, Jane Austen's own favourite. *Sir Charles Grandison* was a book which took a model gentleman as its central character and through him presented an ideal code of conduct for civilised bourgeois relationships. A whole range of novels that dealt with manners followed in Richardson's wake, and *Sense and Sensibility* owes a great deal to this tradition. Jane Austen extends the scope of this often didactic fiction by using her observation of manners to examine degrees of gentility and to suggest something of what that problematic concept involves. She is therefore particularly careful to distinguish between good manners (thoughtful consideration of others) and mere etiquette (a slavish following of rules). Lady Middleton, for example, is the personification of formal elegance. Her behaviour is entirely governed by her consciousness of the proprieties. In London she is loath to offer hospitality to the Dashwoods in case her impromptu party is frowned upon by the fashionable élite. This sort of adherence to etiquette is presented as hollow. The forms of her behaviour have no deeper basis and can be no substitute for her utter lack of human sympathy. Conversely, Jane Austen forgives Mrs Jennings her vulgar manner, her lapses in speech, her loud laugh and her often untimely jokes because her intentions spring from a real kindness of heart and a compassionate interest in others.

Jane Austen presents us with a succession of levels of courtesy in *Sense and Sensibility* that are intended to tell us something about social ethics. Students sometimes accuse her of snobbery because she is so insistent on class boundaries, but wealth and social position are for Jane Austen no guarantee of gentility. Mrs Ferrars, the most ostentatiously affluent and one of the most powerful characters in the novel, is also one of those capable of the greatest moral grossness. At the John Dashwoods' formally correct dinner party in Chapter 34, where 'everything bespoke the Mistress's inclination for shew and the Master's ability to support it', we are treated to a display of deliberate rudeness when Mrs Ferrars insults Elinor by making disparaging remarks about the pair of decorative firescreens. It is central to Jane Austen's method (and incidentally an ironic reversal of the procedure of sentimentalism) that apparent trivia are invested with moral status. Here, Mrs Ferrars' comments about the firescreens, as she tries to mortify Elinor, are a case in point. The merest fragment of discourtesy is sufficient to reveal an entire moral character.

The emphasis on the significance of social detail is intrinsic to Jane Austen's realist vision. It relates to the charge sometimes levelled against her that her world is narrow in its obsession with minutiae. As part of her deflation of fictional romance, Jane Austen presents us with a world that is in many ways its precise opposite. She wants to make it clear that the lives of most middle-class young women are not carried out in exotic locations but in homely drawing-rooms; nor do they consist of dramatic events, but of family quarrels and small talk with acquaintances. For most of us, as for the characters in *Sense and Sensibility*, the fabric of life is made up of mundane incidents, trivial conversations and ordinary people like ourselves. Yet it is these small incidents that furnish the excitement of individual existence, that provide the emotional fluctuations and determine its moral dimension.

We need to recognise that the particular instances of etiquette cited by Jane Austen are, like the world she describes, used to denote a much wider area of significance. In commenting on the rules that, for example, dictate that a young lady must not write to a young gentleman unless they have announced their engagement, Jane Austen is describing how outward formalities help to define a clearly understood structure of social relations, and how any disruption of that structure can have damaging and far-reaching consequences. Marianne's disregard for the minutiae of social observance does more than create a rather embarassing situation for her. It relates crucially to a perception of self which sets personal desire above all else. We need to be alert to the fact that Willoughby, who should know better, encourages Marianne to flout the conventions. In the pursuit of his own pleasure, he is prepared to put her reputation at risk. Manners form a highly complicated system of signs, and Willoughby and Marianne's flagrant behaviour indicates to onlookers something which is not true, namely that the couple are going to be married. The resulting uncertainty about Marianne's status creates confusion and awkwardness for her family, and Marianne's subsequent personal crisis when Willoughby disowns her becomes a matter of public notice and brings distress to her mother and sister. Society is a force that cannot be ignored, and individual wishes need to take into account the procedures agreed by decorum. A quite different illustration of this can be seen at Mrs Jennings' house when Marianne refuses to enter into polite conversation because she finds conformity to false patterns of behaviour dishonest. The result is an extra burden for her sister, as Elinor must struggle to compensate for Marianne's incivility.

In her analysis of social behaviour and its effects, Jane Austen gradually reveals a power structure where communal and personal values are often in conflict. The plot of *Sense and Sensibility* demonstrates how individuals are dependent on the goodwill of their communities, and how arbitrary that goodwill can be. The main action of the novel is framed by two events which show this. When Mrs Dashwood and her daughters are evicted from Norland, they find another home only through the charity of Sir John Middleton. Similarly, at the end of the book, Elinor and Edward are reliant on Colonel Brandon's generosity in providing them with Delaford Parsonage as a means of income. Edward's disinheritance is similarly arbitrary. His mother has no real cause for rejecting him in favour of his brother, and he is never reinstated. Edward's code, based on honour and personal merit, is different from his mother's, based on money and social ambition, but it is she who holds the purse strings, and who can determine his future. Again and again Jane Austen reveals the injustices at the heart of the social system. In her portrayal of a realistic world, virtue is not inevitably rewarded. It is for example the unworthy Lucy Steele who gains fortune and favour, but it is she who least deserves them.

Jane Austen is deeply interested in the mechanics of social survival and she depicts a world where for some people, particularly women, this is a difficult process. We need to remember that she was writing at a time when the position of women in society was much more precarious than it is today and social compliance became a necessary form of protection. Marriage was really the only career available to middle-class young ladies, who were otherwise dependent on their relatives for support. The Dashwood girls, although of good family, have no substantial income of their own. John Dashwood's concern that his sisters should find rich husbands springs partly from his worry that otherwise he might be expected to look after them. Frequently in Jane Austen's novels, we are made aware of the desperation behind a girl's desire to marry. Anne Steele is a comic but pathetic instance of a woman who fears she is a social failure because she has not found a husband. I am not suggesting that Jane Austen is mercenary in her attitude. She is highly critical of women like Lucy who marry purely for financial gain, but she does realise that economic security is an issue that cannot be ignored, and that social approval is inextricably linked with behaviour.

In *Sense and Sensibility*, relations between unmarried women and men are governed by strict rules that cover many minor forms of social activity: dancing, letter-writing, accepting gifts, visiting alone. Jane Austen stresses that the codes of etiquette both control and protect young women from dangerous situations. When Marianne transgresses the unwritten laws, she puts herself at risk. The story of her relationship with Willoughby, with its corollary of the story of the seduced and abandoned Eliza Williams, alerts us to the potential dangers that Marianne could encounter. Jane Austen is not making a simple point here of 'don't trust men', but a more complex social one. She shows that women need to understand their fragile position and cannot afford to be unguarded in their social behaviour.

If we follow through Jane Austen's reasoning and her analysis of social codes, we can begin to see that she is presenting us with two seemingly opposing views. Through her investigation of sensibility she asserts the importance of natural feeling with its unpredictable gusts of sympathy. Simultaneously, she writes about the importance of controlling the expression of feeling for the sake of social and moral order.

3.3 GROWING UP

Growing up is a central issue in *Sense and Sensibility*. In many ways, it brings together the two other topic headings in this section, individual feeling and social behaviour. Character is perceived as operating in two dimensions, the inner life of private feeling and the outer life of public affairs, and Jane Austen sees the process of growing up as essentially one of learning how to adapt individual impulses to established ideas of social forms.

Once again, the theme is expanded primarily through the presentation of Marianne Dashwood as an adolescent who makes mistakes about the nature of the world around her. (Remember that she is only just seventeen.) It is characteristic of the eighteenth century and of Jane Austen's approach in particular, that growing up is closely associated with the idea of moral and social education. Although Jane Austen portrays Marianne as a character who makes many errors, she never condemns her outright. She does not question her fundamental integrity, but shows her rather as a character whose sense of her own identity is confused. Marianne's impetuousness, her idealism and her outspokenness – all of which are emphasised in the first half of the novel – are qualities that Jane Austen suggests are normal products of youthful energy, and they have their own imaginative appeal. 'There is something so amiable in the prejudices of a young mind, that one is sorry to see them give way to the reception of more general opinions,' says Colonel Brandon in Chapter 11. Yet Marianne must learn to accommodate her own opinions to the inflexible standards of the society around her if she wants to avoid getting hurt. As Elinor replies,

> There are inconveniences attending such feelings as Marianne's, which all the charms of enthusiasm and ignorance of the world cannot atone for. Her systems have the unfortunate tendency of setting propriety at nought; and a better acquaintance with the world is what I look forward to as her greatest possible advantage.

Marianne's journey to understanding this is a painful one, but it is a necessary preparation for her ultimate marriage, the state which for Jane Austen's heroines represents the mature integration of personal emotion into an accepted social format, and with which Marianne is rewarded at the end of the novel.

Jane Austen uses the subject of Marianne's personal growth to enquire into a topic that was a popular debating point in eighteenth-century discussions about ideas, that is, the vexed question of the relationship between nature and art. Marianne's natural impulses, however intrinsically admirable, need to be fashioned and controlled by a conscious effort. For instance, the novel makes frequent reference to the virtue of honesty, a concept that Marianne at first vehemently defends at all costs. 'It was impossible for her to say what she did not feel, however trivial the occasion', remarks Jane Austen in Chapter 21, going on to demonstrate that deceit is sometimes a social necessity, for 'upon Elinor therefore the whole task of telling lies when politeness required it, always fell'. Marianne's perfectionism must be modified to the requirements of an imperfect world and compromise is one of the hard lessons she is called on to learn.

It is important to Jane Austen's meaning that Marianne is shown, not in isolation, but as part of a close-knit family unit. Her mistakes are highlighted by the maturity of her elder sister, Elinor, and by the raw childishness of her younger sister, Margaret. Margaret's embarrassingly juvenile behaviour in Chapter 12, for example, when she blurts out half-truths about her sisters' romances, helps to put Marianne's more developed sensitivity into perspective. For it is the state of adolescence that is under scrutiny here, as being a time of life when human beings are particularly vulnerable. Jane Austen is interested in the growth to independence and the adolescent mind is seen as being midway between the state of childhood protection and a full self-awareness. In order to show this change taking place, Jane Austen moves the Dashwood sisters to London. This journey away from the heroines' home reflects a metaphorical journey to self-knowledge and it is a motif we find in several of Jane Austen's novels. In considering how character develops, Jane Austen examines carefully the nature and extent of parental influence. She shows her heroines' relationship with their parents or guardians, and then, in almost all her books, she sends them on a trip to another, unfamiliar location where they face a moral and/or emotional crisis and where they are forced to demonstrate self-reliance. For Marianne in *Sense and Sensibility*, this crisis occurs at the ball in London where she confronts Willoughby, an incident which pushes her to readjust radically her views on life and on love, as well as her understanding of her own identity.

It is also typical of Jane Austen that most of her young heroines have either dead, absent or inadequate parents, and thus the process of their psychological development is more sharply defined. In *Sense and Sensibility*, Marianne's father is dead and her mother is fallible. Marianne's relationship with her mother in fact is seen as a crucial factor in the formation of her character, as Jane Austen weighs the relative effects of genetics, environment and upbringing on the growing personality. Marianne and her mother are described as resembling one another temperamentally and Mrs Dashwood's love and care have nurtured Marianne in an affectionate home that has brought out the best in her. Jane Austen is also careful to point out, however, that Mrs Dashwood's attitudes to her daughters often lack a sense of her own responsibilities as a mother. Parents must take their duties seriously, and Mrs Dashwood's unchecked sympathy for Marianne emerges as a form of indulgence, harmful rather than beneficial because it has given her a disproportionate view of self. Encouraging Marianne to give way to her emotions whenever she feels like it, Mrs Dashwood has failed to create the proper conditions for her daughter's growth to social maturity, and it is only when Marianne leaves her mother behind that she can achieve a clearer perspective on her own actions. Similarly, Mrs Dashwood errs in her treatment of Elinor, whose temperament is unlike her own, and whom she consequently fails to notice is in need of maternal comfort and support.

The emphasis on correct guidance and its effect on character is not confined to the portrayal of Marianne. Willoughby's casual and damaging behaviour is explained by Jane Austen as stemming from 'too early an independence and its consequent habits of idleness, dissipation and luxury' (ch. 44). Note that she does not excuse Willoughby, but she does place him firmly in context, as a responsive and impressionable boy who has been deprived of proper moral direction, with the result that his abilities have been thwarted. Adolescence is again perceived as the vital stage in personal development, the time when the acquisition of independence has to be most delicately managed. Continually, Jane Austen reminds us of the external or environmental factors imposing on what she terms 'natural' abilities. Even the reprehensible Lucy Steele, 'naturally clever', is an object of some pity for having missed out on the advantages of a reasonable education and upbringing.

It is unusual for Jane Austen to write about very young children in her books, but in *Sense and Sensibility* she does introduce several instances of children's behaviour. Sometimes, as in the cases of John Dashwood's son, Harry, or Lady Middleton's William, these are used to strengthen the family patterns of the novel and the sense of continuing generations. However, she is also concerned to point out the destructive impact of too much parental fondness on an unformed personality. She relates this to the question of what constitutes 'nature' before it has been subjected to the process of discipline and education. Jane Austen's fictional children notably fail to conform to the image of docile innocence that sentimentalists believed was their natural state. The Middleton children in Chapter 21 are noisy, wild and uncivilised, meddlesome interruptions into adult life. The language used by the Steeles and Lady Middleton to describe the three-year-old Annamaria, 'sweet', 'gentle' and 'quiet', is at odds with her

conduct, as she screams and yells, knowing that she can mani-
pulate the adults who attend to her. Jane Austen is reacting here
to the popular 'romantic' theory of childhood as a time of
innocence and freshness of insight, a time when instinctive response was thought to be at its purest, uncorrupted by contact with
the world.

4 TECHNIQUES

4.1 A NOTE ABOUT THE COMIC FORM

In reading Jane Austen's novels, we need to bear in mind that above all Jane Austen is a comic writer. By saying this, I am not implying that the subjects treated within the text are light-hearted: the preceding discussions of Section 3 show that Jane Austen deals with very serious issues indeed. Rather when we talk about comedy, we are usually referring to the distanced stance of the writer who controls the characters and plot in such a way that the underlying seriousness does not become too intense. So in looking at the techniques used by Jane Austen in *Sense and Sensibility*, we need to appreciate the demands of the comic vision that informs the whole. Not only is *Sense and Sensibility* a marvellously funny book with its acid ironic commentary and its hilarious portraits of ridiculously affected characters, but it is a work conceived within an artistic framework that imposes its own rules, and this is something more difficult to grasp.

Jane Austen is a realist. She writes about a familiar and fully detailed localised environment and she faces the problems of her society and her characters without flinching from unpleasant truths. However, we must not confuse the term 'realist' with 'real', for comedy inevitably involves a degree of artificiality. Jane Austen makes no attempt to convince us of the authenticity of her world. We know that Elinor and Marianne are fictitious beings and are therefore quite prepared to suspend our disbelief when we read about their adventures. The consistency of comic tone and the adherence to certain literary conventions ensures that we know that, despite several setbacks along the way, a happy ending for all the main characters is guaranteed. Jane Austen deliberately fashions her ideas and characters into a highly self-conscious scheme and in this respect she is a most sophisticated writer, aware all the time that the comic world of fiction contains its own rules and must retain its own sense of artistic logic to be fully effective.

4.2 PLOT AND STRUCTURE

When *Sense and Sensibility* was first published, it was divided into three volumes, and these suggest the division of the work into three separate stages. The first volume (up to Chapter 22) brings us to the first major obstacle to Elinor's future happiness, Lucy Steele's announcement of her engagement to Edward Ferrars. A feeling of suspense is created which leads us on to Volume 2. This concluded with another set-back to the Dashwoods, as the Steele sisters are welcomed into John Dashwood's home (at the end of Chapter 36) and seem to be usurping the place that Elinor and Marianne by rights should occupy. Each of these first two volumes ends at a low point in the Dashwood girls' fortunes, and we can make a progressive comparison between the two. The third is one of resolution, as the complications and ever-increasing disasters of the first two sections are sorted out, and, with a series of unexpected twists to the action, Jane Austen cleverly brings about the restoration of order and the happy ending we all want.

Even such a simple division as this shows how thoughtfully Jane Austen made the story fit into an ordered form, and indeed when we study any novel properly, we should pay close attention to the way in which an author manages his or her material. In *Sense and Sensibility* this formal organisation is an active agent in the novel's meaning. For *Sense and Sensibility* is an intensively patterned and most carefully structured work, based around a series of ironic oppositions. The book's title, focusing on abstractions, *sense* and *sensibility*, immediately announces the author's interest in working through a scheme of ideas. Yet we must read the title with care. It is not 'sense *or* sensibility' but 'sense *and* sensibility'. The two concepts are not presented, as is sometimes thought, as simple antitheses but as complementary qualities, and this concordance is reflected by their parallel examination in the thematic structure of the text. The novel in fact explores varying notions of *sense* and *sensibility*, subtly refined and developed, so that all the characters and incidents in the book contribute to a process of compositional analysis.

The plot of *Sense and Sensibility* is to some extent an ironic reversal of the plots of traditional romantic fiction, but simultaneously Jane Austen cleverly exploits traditional fictional devices to create her story. Firstly we are offered two figures who might fill the conventional role of heroine. Readers coming to the novel for the first time are commonly betrayed into thinking that Marianne is the emotional centre of attention, and that Elinor is her foil. I would argue that the reverse is the case, and that such a misconception is a stratagem on the part of Jane Austen who deliberately misleads the reader for ironic purposes. Jane Austen wants to disturb our preconceived opinions about *sense* and *sensibility* and about what we expect from a novel, just as she wants to disabuse Marianne of her fixed views on life. Like Marianne, for instance, we too think at first that Willoughby is the hero.

From this starting point, Jane Austen then develops a further series of conventional reversals. So the youthful *ingénue* marries in the end a man who is the exact opposite of her romantic ideal. Not only does Marianne initially view Brandon as a stuffy older man incapable of sensitive feeling, but she marries him without being passionately in love, a total contradiction of the fictional norm. The novel's movement through Marianne thus appears to be towards the assertion of rationalism, giving us a common-sense view of marriage. This movement is subverted, however, by the process of the relationship between Elinor and Edward. They at first seem to be anti-romantic figures, always checking Marianne's extravagant outbursts of feeling (remember the deadpan remarks about dead leaves?). Yet their path towards marriage conforms closely to the plots we find in traditional romance. Let us try to see it in those terms. We have two young lovers (Elinor for all her maturity is only nineteen), parted by a cruel parent who tries to prevent the virtually penniless heroine from marrying the wealthy heir to a fortune. Their love is beset by obstacles, and when they are eventually united, their marriage is patently for love, not money, for Edward has been disinherited. Can you see how the plot itself with its parallel actions relating to the two sisters both disrupts and fulfils our expectations of the progress of romantic narrative?

We can see the same sort of method at work in the development of the girls' male counterparts, whose actions are implicitly measured against those of a model romantic hero. The apparent hero, Willoughby, turns out to be the villain of the piece, and it is the two anti-heroes, Brandon and Edward (who are not just passive appropriate husbands for the Dashwood sisters), who show they are capable of conventionally heroic conduct. Brandon performs the only really melodramatic deed in the book when he challenges Willoughby to a duel, and fights it. Edward resembles the courtly gallant of chivalric romance when he stands up to his mother and maintains his fidelity to Lucy. Note the report of his language in Chapter 37. It is lifted from the romantic stereotype, with its stress on honour, loyalty and adherence to a heroic code. Of course, the episode is given further ironic bite by the fact that Edward cares nothing for Lucy and he defends her under a mistaken understanding of the situation.

The action in this way creates a series of thematic reversals; impulsiveness (in Willoughby) becomes prudence; practical common-sense (in Elinor) becomes sensitivity; gentility (in Lady Middleton) becomes discourtesy; vulgarity (in Mrs Jennings) becomes simple kindness; and so on. The workings of the plot and the various narrative complications serve to blur our sense of clear definition, as different scenes offer us alternative interpretations of these concepts. Look for example at the parallel departures of Brandon and Willoughby from Barton in almost identical circumstances. Willoughby's comments on Brandon in Chapter 13 are used to arouse our suspicions in Chapter 15 about the meanings behind secrecy and silence. The sequence of action is built around confusions, half-truths and misunderstandings. Look at Jane Austen's management of the episode concerning the ring that Edward wears. We are allowed to be in error and are not undeceived until Elinor herself is told the truth.

The characters in *Sense and Sensibility* are conceived in terms of the contribution they make to an overall sense of pattern. We are supplied with two heroines and their analogous love stories which work in tandem. We have alternative versions of a hero figure in Willoughby, Edward and Brandon, all of whom provide mutual points of comparison at different stages in the narrative. Often one enters as the other leaves (see for instance Chapters 15 and 16; and Chapters 32 and 33, where on each occasion after Willoughby's departure, Edward is reintroduced into the story). Jane Austen creates families who form mirror-images of one another. The Ferrars brothers, the Steele sisters, the Jennings daughters (Lady Middleton and Mrs Palmer), reflect the parallelism of the Dashwood girls, as they exhibit aspects of the sense/sensibility division. In all cases, some modification must be made on the part of the reader as to how the concepts of the title are interpreted. In this respect, Edward and Robert Ferrars, for example, change roles, as do Elinor and Marianne. Edward, who seems at first to embody *sense*, ends up acting out a role lifted from sentimental literature, while Robert, who attempts to display his excessive refinement and *sensibility* in his scrupulous choice of toothpick case, is a cold opportunist, who usurps his brother's position.

The scheme is intentionally deceptive. We are constantly misled as to the roles the characters are required to perform. Willoughby, for example, who is presented in the beginning as the embodiment of open-hearted spontaneity turns out to be motivated by material advantage, making a mercenary marriage despite his professions of love. Similarly Marianne, determined to behave instinctively, finds herself acting according to a predetermined system that specifies what poetry she should read, what music she ought to play, what landscape she should admire. Gradually our ability to define the terms *sense* and *sensibility* begins to fade, as the concepts are revealed as more subtle than we had at first imagined. Ask yourselves how this is done. We move as readers from certainty to uncertainty as the categorisation clouds, but do we then come to a fuller understanding? The uses of comparison in *Sense and Sensibility* are almost limitless. It is as if Jane Austen is moving her characters as in a formal dance to create innumerable combinations which highlight one another. At different times in the novel, Marianne is contrasted with Elinor and with Lucy, while together the Dashwood sisters are measured both against the Steele sisters and against Mrs Jennings' daughters. Similarly, Mrs Dashwood is implicitly compared with other mothers in the text: Mrs Ferrars, Lady Middleton, Mrs Jennings and Fanny Dashwood. Sometimes the nature of these comparisons is surprising, as Jane Austen reveals similarities between characters who seem most unlike. The resemblance between Marianne and Mrs Jennings is perhaps the most obvious example, but there are others too. How many can you find?

The arrangement of character and action is deliberately formal and this formality is integral to the design of the whole. For *Sense and Sensibility* announces its own status as an artistic construct all the way through. Being a novel that makes such self-conscious reference to other novels it can hardly do otherwise. The ending is particularly mannered, calling attention to its own artistry. Note how neatly the story is fitted into exactly fifty chapters. Chapter 50 itself reinforces the symmetry that has been a major structuring device of the novel, through Jane Austen's obvious skill in tying up loose ends. The various couples are united, all earlier problems are tidily resolved with rewards and punishments summarily dealt out, and Jane Austen gives the conclusion an air of comic detachment that makes the artificial nature of the whole quite explicit.

The progression to order relates centrally to the earlier action of the novel which evolves through a cleverly structured pattern of plans and accidents. An understanding of the process of the narrative relies on recognising the way in which Jane Austen uses repeated motifs of surprise and disruption to a regulated scheme. Frequently we find that plans are thwarted by unexpected occurrences, from Mr Dashwood's death, through Marianne's accidental fall, to the cancelled visit to Whitwell and Edward's unexpected arrival at Barton (on two occasions). Just as Jane Austen creates a meaningful tension between varying notions of *sense* and *sensibility*, so the form of the novel re-enacts that tension by moving between order and disturbance in its very action. Continually Jane Austen suggests that rationalism and logic are fallible, subject to unforeseen emotional impulses that undermine their own sense of control. One good example of this is the scene when Willoughby arrives without warning at Cleveland and Elinor, despite her reservations about his treatment of Marianne, finds herself responding to his charm. When the novel's ending draws attention to its own ability to command events, it is inviting us to be sceptical of its validity. We should ask ourselves how far the closure corresponds to the thematic resolution of harmony and a belief in the establishment of order, and how far it questions the truth of that order. This is a difficult question to answer. Whatever conclusion we come to – even if we admit that perhaps it's doing

both things simultaneously – by asking the question, we acknowledge the importance of the plot and structure in trying to understand the meaning of the novel. *Sense and Sensibility* is not a mechanical text that can be assimilated at one reading, but a complex interplay of ideas, and it is by looking carefully at the structure of the novel that we come closer to understanding its ambiguities.

4.3 METHODS OF CHARACTERISATION

'It is to express character,' said the twentieth-century writer, Virginia Woolf, 'not to preach doctrines, sing songs or celebrate the glories of the British Empire, that the form of the novel . . . has been evolved.' For Virginia Woolf, as for many writers, character was the most important element in a novel, and many readers today would still agree with her. It is the human dimension in a book which focuses our attention, helps us to identify with the situations and is usually what engages our sympathy. When we read Jane Austen's fiction, even though it was written nearly two hundred years ago, we have no difficulty in recognising among her characters types of human beings who are familiar to us from our own experience. It is the variety of human nature, in its essentials unchanging, which provides Jane Austen with the basic material for the examination of her ideas.

If we think about it, however, it is perhaps odd that we recognise Jane Austen's people so intimately, for she hardly ever gives us any physical descriptions to go by. We know that *Marianne Dashwood* is exceptionally pretty that 'her skin was very brown' and that she has dark eyes, but the impression we gain of her life and energy comes from her speech and actions rather than from any factual details. Jane Austen might *tell* us that her characters are tall, good-looking or elegant, but she does not attempt to draw any physical portraits. How then is it that we do gain such a distinct impression of their individuality?

The answer must lie partly in what I have just said about Marianne's speech and actions. All Jane Austen's novels, but *Sense and Sensibility* in particular, create characters through dramatic means. Jane Austen herself loved theatre, and play-acting was a favourite form of entertainment in the Austen family circle. Jane

Austen's fine dramatic sense permeates *Sense and Sensibility*, much of which reads like a rather wordy play, with great reliance on dialogue. Personalities reveal themselves through their speech, and their language is highly idiosyncratic. Often we don't really need to be told who is speaking in order to identify the characters involved. Let's look at the following passage as an example

> Nay, my dear, I'm sure I don't pretend to say that there an't. I'm sure there's a vast many smart beaux in Exeter; but you know, how could I tell what smart beaux there might be about Norland; and I was only afraid the Miss Dashwoods might find it dull at Barton, if they had not so many as they used to have. But perhaps you young ladies may not care about the beaux, and had as lief be without them as with them. For my part, I think they are vastly agreeable, provided they dress smart and behave civil. But I can't bear to see them dirty and nasty. Now, there's Mr Rose at Exeter, a prodigious smart young man, quite a beau, clerk to Mr Simpson you know, and yet if you do but meet him of a morning, he is not fit to be seen.—I suppose your brother was quite a beau, Miss Dashwood, before he married, as he was so rich? (Ch. 21)

Here *Anne Steele* is sharply defined. Her use of language is careless, ungrammatical and intended to show up her vulgarity of mind. She is obsessed with *beaux*. Her vocabulary is limited and clumsy – she uses the word 'smart' four times in this brief extract, but what does it mean exactly? I think you'll agree that by the time she has reached the end of the paragraph it has become an empty cliché.

This sort of dramatic representation works especially well with the comic characters of the novel, several of whom border on farce in the absurd near monologues that Jane Austen writes for them. *Robert Ferrars'* disquisition on cottages (Ch. 36) and *John Dashwood*'s account of the 'shocking discovery' of Edward's engagement (Ch. 37) are two beautiful examples of this self-revelatory method of characterisation.

With her more serious characters though, Jane Austen's technique is slightly different, for often those people whom Jane Austen presents as experiencing profound emotion are those who are most inept at expressing themselves. *Edward Ferrars*, for example, conspicuously lacks verbal fluency and is criticised by Marianne for his poor performance when reading aloud. 'Spiritless and tame' (ch. 3) are the words she uses to condemn him. Readers who sympathise with Marianne's opinion might call Edward an inadequate hero for the novel, not up to Elinor's stature. What do you think about this? Certainly Jane Austen's male characters are never as fully realised as her women. She herself was determined to write about only what she knew intimately. When her niece wrote to ask her aunt's advice about a novel she wanted to set in Ireland, Jane Austen's advice was simple. 'Do not set your story in Ireland if you have not been there. You will be in danger of making false representations.' Working on the same principle, Jane Austen in her own novels never shows men in conversation alone together, for she would not have known what they spoke about when women were not present. So, in *Sense and Sensibility* Edward is presented in rather oblique ways, largely through other people's reports of him. Marianne, Elinor, Mrs Dashwood and Lucy are some of those who tell us what they think. By this means, the reader is not allowed to forget Edward, but he might seem a rather shadowy figure, filtered through second-hand comments. Just one scene, however, does seem to stand apart from this and to indicate the degree of psychological realism Jane Austen can bring to non-central characters. The scene I am referring to occurs in Chapter 48 when Edward, in the grip of strong emotion, automatically picks up a pair of scissors and cuts their sheath to pieces without realising it. Focusing on the external action, Jane Austen here reveals the state of mind beneath.

The majority of the characters emerge through the observation of speech and mannerisms but one important exception to this must be *Elinor*. In considering how characters are drawn in a novel, we need to take into account the narrative stance of the author and her position *vis-à-vis* her creations. Most of the time in *Sense and Sensibility*, Jane Austen is outside her characters, providing satiric comments on their actions which set up the dramatic conversations and determine our objective responses. In the case of Elinor, however, the ironic viewpoint is largely absent. the presentation is much more subjective and we are encouraged to identify closely with her perceptions. Frequently we can take her remarks as an extension of the author's own voice. When Elinor notices that *Lady Middleton*'s 'reserve was a mere calmness of manner with which sense had nothing to do' (Ch. 11), we accept this judgement as authoritative, because there is no distinction made between Jane Austen's tone and Elinor's.

For a heroine, *Elinor* might be thought unusually quiet. Like Edward she is often marked by her silence, for instead of concentrating on her outward behaviour, Jane Austen tends to dramatise her internal condition. In order to do this effectively, she employs a technique that we normally associate with much more modern writers. In the following extract from Chapter 23 you can see how gradually we are absorbed into Elinor's consciousness as she mulls over what Lucy Steele has just told her about Edward.

> Her resentment of such behaviour, her indignation at having been its dupe, for a short time made her feel only for herself; but other ideas, other considerations soon arose. Had Edward been intentionally deceiving her? Had he feigned a regard for her which he did not feel? Was his engagement to Lucy, an engagement of the heart? No; whatever it might once have been, she could not believe it such at present. His affection was all her own. She could not be deceived in that. Her mother, sisters, Fanny, all had been conscious of his regard for her at Norland; it was not an illusion of her own vanity. He certainly loved her.

The first sentence is written as we would expect in the third person, but then the structure changes and the next few shorter sentences move us into Elinor's mind. The author's voice is absent and we are allowed direct access to Elinor's thoughts, following her arguments as they would suggest themselves to her, and reproducing the processes of her mental workings. This technique can be termed free indirect speech. The sentences are still written in the past tense and framed by the implicit third person viewpoint of the first sentence to which the passage ultimately returns, but the words and phrases are Elinor's, questioning, trying to understand what she has heard, and are far removed from the omniscient, controlled and detached persona we have come to identify as the author.

In *Sense and Sensibility* Jane Austen carefully establishes a moral world in which to place her characters whom we are invited to judge according to an ideal behavioural standard. Characters are thus conceived in evaluative terms and their dramatisation takes place in a context of values which asks us to measure their actions. Look for instance at the introduction to *Marianne* in Chapter 1. 'She was sensible and clever, but eager in everything; her sorrows, her joys could have no moderation. She was generous, amiable, interesting; she was everything but prudent.' The features that Jane Austen mentions here all refer to abstract qualities and the subsequent realisation of Marianne is an active demonstration of these terms. We should note incidentally that they are all admirable: 'sensible', 'clever', 'generous', 'amiable', 'interesting' – so that the word 'everything' coming at the end of this list indicates a positive not a negative feature, and the lack of prudence suggests a deficiency that can be remedied rather than any evil tendency of character.

We have to remember in thinking about the characterisation in this book that Jane Austen was extremely conscious of the accepted types of fictional characters found in the pages of the popular novels of her day. I have suggested in section 4.1 that the characters in some way all relate to the sense and sensibility theme, but we should not take the people in *Sense and Sensibility* as either stereotypes or as mere ciphers, theoretical embodiments of ideas. They are all provided with a human personality – even those who are quite sketchily drawn such as *Sir John Middleton* or *Mrs Palmer* – and they refuse to fit into any preconceived mould. *Willoughby* for instance is based on a type of model hero in the first part of the book and on an image of that stock villain, the vile seducer, in the second part, but his individual nature evades either of these narrow definitions. The scene with Elinor at Cleveland (Ch. 44) gives him a convincing background of social and psychological motivation that prevents our responding to him as some sort of cardboard cut-out.

Mrs Jennings is another such example of Jane Austen's revision of stereotypes. On her first appearance we are tempted to dismiss Mrs Jennings as a caricature of a good-humoured, vulgar, gossipy old woman, but as the novel develops and the character unfolds, we have to acknowledge that she is more complex than this. Through her, Jane Austen is making points about kindness and its relation to our assessment of behaviour, and we find that Mrs Jennings has an important part to play in the exploration of values that the novel establishes through its characters.

4.4 LANGUAGE AND STYLE

Jane Austen's art is essentially one of economy. She includes nothing that is extraneous to her purpose and she makes the language of her novels work hard for her. Correspondingly, Jane Austen's reader also has to work hard in order to extract the full meaning of her words and phrases which are often used to carry a resonance extending far beyond their existing surface simplicity.

A term that will inevitably recur in any discussion of Jane Austen's style is 'irony'. What exactly is meant by this? Technically, irony refers to a device whereby a statement is invested with a level of meaning not immediately apparent and not straightforward. Jane Austen is very fond of this technique and exploits it to produce some of her most brilliant comic effects. The first sentence of Chapter 50 in *Sense and Sensibility*, for instance, relies on our being able to read the implications behind the words.

> After a proper resistance on the part of Mrs Ferrars, just so violent and so steady as to preserve her from that reproach which she always seemed fearful of incurring, the reproach of being too amiable, Edward was admitted to her presence, and pronounced to be again her son.

To appreciate the full force of this, we need to be alert to the ambiguities it contains. What does the word 'proper' mean here, for example? Jane Austen is not simply reporting Mrs Ferrars' acceptance of Edward, but is inviting us to see her as a spiteful, intolerant and thoroughly nasty woman, although she never actually says this directly. Yet the formality of much of the language, 'preserve', 'admitted', 'presence', 'pronounced' is clearly quite inappropriate for talking about a mother and son relationship. The word 'amiable' too comes as a surprise. Is Jane Austen really saying that Mrs Ferrars deliberately wants people to think of her as unpleasant?

We should recognise that, for Jane Austen, irony is much more than a clever linguistic tool. Her perception of ambiguities informs her entire vision of life, and her novels are conceived with a continual sense of the possibilities of alternative interpretations. We have already seen how this works with regard to both the action and the characters in *Sense and Sensibility*, where nothing is as it seems. In addition, we must understand that the style in which the novel is written reinforces this sense of complexity at every stage.

Irony works as a corrective force and Jane Austen establishes an implicit norm right at the beginning of the book against which all deviation can be measured. We have noted her fondness for abstract nouns in the section on characterisation and we can see how this sets up a standard of moral value that helps to direct the response of the reader. The ironies often appear within a context of plain statements of fact. Let us look at the following as an example.

> Edward had no turn for great men or barouches. All his wishes centred in domestic comfort and the quiet of private life. Fortunately he had a brother who was more promising. (Ch. 2)

The tone of the final sentence here is clearly at variance with the directness of the two that precede it. The contrast between the material 'barouches' and the intangible 'domestic comfort' suggests an evaluative contrast between frivolity and permanence that prevents us from taking the 'fortunately' and the 'promising' at face value. Jane Austen thus manages to point up snobbery and the false values of the Ferrars family.

As an omniscient narrator, Jane Austen determines the frame of reference for our reading and makes assumptions that we are expected to share. Consider this next sentence. 'She had an excellent heart; her disposition was affectionate, and her feelings were strong' is how Elinor is introduced. The sentence is brief, direct and lucid. The devastating description of Lucy Steele works on similar lines.

> She was ignorant and illiterate, and her deficiency of all mental improvement, her want of information in the most common particular, could not be concealed from Miss Dashwood, in spite of her continual endeavours to appear to advantage. (Ch. 22)

The abstract terms in both these cases relate to moral and ethical properties, and as readers we are asked to participate actively in the text by exercising our own sense of moral judgement, a crucial piece of equipment for any Jane Austen reader. In these two sentences, Jane Austen's tone is one of complete authority. In reading, we are invited to accept without question the implied value system, and are intended to decry ignorance and illiteracy just as much as we have to admire affection and strong feeling. Only when these standards have been established can we feel confident about enjoying (and condemning) the spectacle of, say, John Dashwood arguing away his sister's income.

In the spare commentary of Jane Austen's world, we find that what is omitted is often as important as what is there. 'Sir John was a sportsman, Lady Middleton a mother,' states Jane Austen tersely. 'He hunted and shot, and she humoured her children.' This is sufficient to sum up their characters and to expose the paucity of their interests (and note the moral weighting attached to the word 'humoured'). Jane Austen organises her phrases stylishly. The antithetical structure of the text as a whole is reflected in the syntax of individual sentences such as these, many of which in this novel are characterised by balance and symmetry.

The comic style of the novel covers a great range, varying from the lighthearted enjoyment of folly for its own sake, to a more serious and incisive tone. One critic, D. W. Harding, termed Jane Austen's style as being one of 'regulated hatred', and we can see how she came to deserve that epithet when we observe the controlled but often devastating verbal attacks she mounts on those she despises. The description of Robert Ferrars, as possessing 'a person and face of strong, natural, sterling insignificance' (Ch. 33) gains its force from the positioning of the last word, produced unexpectedly from the line of qualifying and normally approving adjectives.

Frequently, Jane Austen allows the point of view to shift suddenly. A character might make an assertion which she then dismantles by a swift dry comment in her own voice, or she exploits the discrepancy in tones between her characters. When Marianne exclaims rapturously over thoughts of autumnal beauty at Norland, her romantic outpourings are summarily undermined by Elinor's laconic remark, 'It is not everyone . . . who has your passion for dead leaves' (Ch. 16).

However, language in *Sense and Sensibility* is not just an agent of communication. It becomes a subject in its own right and takes on the status of a central topic in a novel which enquires searchingly into the nature of personal expression. Marianne alerts us to the problematic nature of language when she admits to difficulties in finding words appropriate to her feelings. 'I detest jargon of every kind', she tells Elinor and Edward, 'and sometimes I have kept my feelings to myself, because I could find no language to describe them in but what was worn and hackneyed out of all sense and meaning' (Ch. 18). It is precisely the sort of clichés that Marianne wishes to avoid that we find dominating the speech of those characters who are least genuine in their professions of feeling. Jane Austen has great fun with burlesque of current idioms in the speeches of Lucy and Anne Steele and Robert Ferrars, who are all guilty of misapplying the jargon of romantic sensibility. Their carelessness with language is equivalent to a moral exposure as they unwittingly reveal their insensitivity.

It is conversely the most feeling characters who are particularly wary of language, conscious of both its limitations and its hidden dangers. The language of Colonel Brandon, for example, is highly restrained. His comments are often terse or non-committal. Remember his refusal to explain his sudden departure for London. Fluency itself indeed is treated with great suspicion. Willoughby's readiness to speak whatever the occasion is a gift mistakenly admired by Marianne, whose own hasty language can also create embarrassment, as when she speaks 'inconsiderately' about the ring that Edward wears. In fact one of the most difficult lessons Marianne has to learn is how to curb her tongue. The cult of sensibility paid great attention to the expressive powers of language, and in *Sense and Sensibility* Jane Austen wants to show how this can be abused. Marianne's fondness for extremes in language tells us that she has adopted unthinkingly the values they encode, while characters who rely on sentimental cliché expose their own lack of originality. 'What a delightful room this is!' exclaims Mrs Palmer on her entrance to Barton Cottage. 'I never saw anything so charming! . . . I always thought it such a sweet place, ma'am' (turning to Mrs Dashwood) 'but you have made it so charming! Only look sister how delightful everything is!' The repetition of the already bland terms, 'delightful', 'charming', strips them totally of meaning, and the uniform intensity of tone, denoted by all those exclamation marks, devalues itself and makes it clear to the reader that such undiscriminating appreciation is worthless.

Sense and Sensibility was originally conceived as a novel composed in letters, and the advantages of this technique still survive, albeit marginally, in the final text. The exchange of letters between Marianne and Willoughby in Chapter 29 demonstrates two styles of writing which are dramatic evidence of the personalities of the correspondents, but which also serve as a comment on the variables that determine meaning. Marianne's letters are informal, frank and personal. The feelings that inspire them are apparent to all and they disclose much more about the relationship between the two than the words alone denote. Style here *is* meaning, as it is the assumption of intimacy which permits the casual tone, the short sentences and the familiar questions. Willoughby's letter, in contrast, employs verbal forms that are intended to deny intimacy and to hurt Marianne. There is a significant discrepancy between the surface value of his words, which conform exactly to standard expressions of civility, and the messages they transmit. Jane Austen is an immensely subtle artist and her flexibility of style is always purposefully directed. Lucy's letter in Chapter 38 is a *tour de force* on the part of Jane Austen as the language is most carefully turned so as to convey different information to its different recipients, while simultaneously confirming our impression of Lucy as crudely manipulative.

Such dualities of language are fully exploited in the scenes between Lucy and Elinor, where often the messages flying between the two women are virtually independent of the terms they use to express themselves. In Chapter 35, for example, their words remain polite and controlled, but there is a subtext of mutually understood hostility, as Elinor and Lucy engage in an undeclared sparring match over Edward's affections. Jane Austen makes her language work overtime. She understands the impact of minute modulations in tone and unearths the existence of levels of covert meaning. In *Sense and Sensibility* she uses these techniques, not just for dramatic or comic effects but to investigate the actual mechanics of communication itself.

5 SPECIMEN PASSAGE
AND COMMENTARY

5.1 SPECIMEN PASSAGE

To understand Jane Austen's art in *Sense and Sensibility*, we need to be exceptionally sensitive to nuances of language. Because Jane Austen deliberately restricts her focus, every detail has to be used purposefully. Nothing is wasted and the impact of the novel relies on the reader's noticing the continual subtle shifts in style and perspective. We can see something of this in an analysis of one short section, although this by no means covers Austen's range in this novel and you will need to analyse for yourself other sections in order to realise the scope of her artistic method. The following passage comes from the end of Chapter 22 (the lines are numbered here for ease of reference) and contains the first important conversation between Elinor and Lucy Steele. Lucy has just told Elinor that for the past four years, she and Edward have been secretly engaged.

'I certainly did not seek your confidence,'
said Elinor; 'but you do me no more than
justice in imagining that I may be depended
on. Your secret is safe with me, but
pardon me if I express some surprise at so   5
unnecessary a communication. You must at
least have felt that my being acquainted
with it could not add to its safety.'
    As she said this, she looked earnestly at
Lucy, hoping to discover something in her   10

countenance, perhaps the falsehood of the
greatest part of what she had been saying;
but Lucy's countenance suffered no change.

'I was afraid you would think I was taking
a great liberty with you,' said she, 'in   15
telling you all this. I have not known you
long to be sure, personally at least, but I
have known you and all your family by
description a great while; and as soon as
I saw you, I felt almost as if you was an   20
old acquaintance. Besides in the present
case I really thought some explanation was due
to you after my making such particular
inquiries about Edward's mother; and I am
so unfortunate that I have not a creature   25
whose advice I can ask. Anne is the only
person that knows of it, and she has no
judgement at all; indeed she does me a great
deal more harm than good, for I am in constant
fear of her betraying me. She does not know   30
how to hold her tongue, as you must perceive,
and I am sure I was in the greatest fright in
the world t'other day when Edward's name was
mentioned by Sir John, lest she should out
with it all. You can't think how much I go   35
through in my mind from it altogether. I
only wonder that I am alive after what I have
suffered for Edward's sake these last four years.
Everything in such suspense and uncertainty, and
seeing him so seldom – we can hardly meet above   40
twice a year. I am sure I wonder my heart is
not quite broke.'

Here she took out her handkerchief, but Elinor
did not feel very compassionate.

'Sometimes,' continued Lucy after wiping her eyes,   45
'I think whether it would not be better for us
both to break off the matter entirely.' As she
said this, she looked directly at her companion.
'But then at other times I have not resolution
enough for it. I cannot bear the thoughts of   50

making him so miserable as I know the very
mention of such a thing would do. And on my own
account too – so dear as he is to me – I don't
think I could be equal to it. What would you
advise me to do in such a case Miss Dashwood? 55
What would you do yourself?'

'Pardon me,' replied Elinor, startled by the
question, 'but I can give you no advice under
such circumstances. Your own judgement must
direct you.' 60

'To be sure,' continued Lucy after a few minutes'
silence on both sides, 'his mother must provide
for him sometime or other, but poor Edward is
so cast down about it! Did not you think him
dreadful low-spirited when he was at Barton? 65
He was so miserable when he left us at Longstaple, to go to you, that I was afraid you
would think him quite ill.'

'Did he come from your uncle's then, when he
visited us?' 70

'Oh! yes, he had been staying a fortnight with
us. Did you think he came directly from town?'

'No,' replied Elinor, most feelingly sensible of
every fresh circumstance in favour of Lucy's
veracity; 'I remember he told us that he had been 75
staying a fortnight with some friends near
Plymouth.' She remembered too her own surprise
at the time, at his mentioning nothing further of
those friends, at his total silence with respect
even to their names. 80

'Did not you think him sadly out of spirits?'
repeated Lucy.

'We did indeed, particularly so when he first
arrived.'

'I begged him to exert himself for fear you 85
should suspect what was the matter; but it
made him so melancholy, not being able to stay
more than a fortnight with us and seeing me so
affected. Poor fellow! I am afraid it is just
the same with him now, for he writes in wretched 90

spirits. I heard from him just before I left
Exeter,' taking a letter from her pocket and
carelessly showing the direction to Elinor. 'You
know his hand, I dare say, a charming one it is;
but that is not written so well as usual. He was   95
tired, I dare say, for he had just filled the
sheet to me as full as possible.'

Elinor saw that it *was* his hand, and she could
doubt no longer. The picture, she had allowed
herself to believe, might have been accidentally   100
obtained; it might not have been Edward's gift;
but a correspondence between them by letter could
subsist only under a positive engagement, could
be authorised by nothing else; for a few moments
she was almost overcome – her heart sank within   105
her, and she could hardly stand; but exertion was
indispensably necessary, and she struggled so
resolutely against the oppression of her feelings
that her success was speedy and for the time
complete.   110

'Writing to each other,' said Lucy, returning
the letter into her pocket, 'is the only comfort
we have in such long separation. Yes, *I* have
one other comfort in his picture; but poor
Edward has not even *that*. If he had but my   115
picture, he says he should be easy. I gave him
a lock of my hair set in a ring when he was at
Longstaple last, and that was some comfort to him,
he said, but not equal to a picture. Perhaps you
might notice the ring when you saw him?'   120

'I did,' said Elinor with a composure of voice
under which was concealed an emotion and distress
beyond anything she had ever felt before. She
was mortified, shocked, confounded.

Fortunately for her, they had now reached the   125
cottage, and the conversation could be continued
no further. After sitting with them a few
minutes, the Miss Steeles returned to the park,
and Elinor was then at liberty to think and be
wretched.   130

5.2 COMMENTARY

This encounter between Elinor and Lucy provides numerous insights into Jane Austen's method. First of all it is a crucial scene in terms of plot. It introduces a complicating action which will not be resolved until the end of the novel: i.e. Lucy's engagement which is an apparently intractable impediment to Elinor's own marriage. The situation established here thus anticipates the Marianne/Willoughby affair to which it forms an ironic parallel. The circumstances of secrecy that surround it are in sharp contrast to the publicity of Marianne's loss of her lover later on. Lucy's revelation also marks the beginning of Elinor's long period of suffering. From this moment until the end of the book, she becomes Jane Austen's true heroine of sensibility, the embodiment of constancy and silent but profound emotion. In terms of character development, it is in this scene that we get the first demonstration of the depth of Elinor's character and the extent of feeling that lies below her apparently calm surface. Her participation in the dialogue is kept to a minimum. When she does speak, her sentences are short and her remarks brief, but her emotions are tumultuous and we are invited to glimpse the hidden levels within her.

By establishing the strength of Elinor's feeling in this section, Jane Austen sets up the central thematic contrast with Marianne, *not* as we might have thought up to this point as a contrast between Elinor's sense and Marianne's sensibility, but rather as a contrast between different types of sensibility, that is different grades of feeling. The language that Jane Austen uses at the end of the scene to describe Elinor's reaction to Lucy, 'mortified, shocked, confounded' (lines 124–30) is direct and authoritative and we are intended to take it seriously.

But this seriousness of tone is the culmination of a scene which starts in a much more openly satiric manner. It is a dramatic scene, like so many in this novel, and the effectiveness of the conversation between the two women rests largely on their individual use of language. Jane Austen develops this episode, as she does virtually every episode in the book, on the basis of an antithesis. Elinor and Lucy embody different social classes, different levels of education, different moral positions, different intellectual abilities and different degrees of sensitivity. Elinor's first speech (lines 1–8) is controlled and considered. The syntax is complex, the construction sophisticated, appropriately reflecting her own intellectual clarity and self-discipline. Note her use of abstract nouns, 'justice', 'surprise', 'communication', 'safety'. Her ability to conceptualise goes with her measured and thoughtful approach to life in general. Her words are chosen with care and economy to point out the inconsistency of Lucy's behaviour.

Lucy's reply which follows (lines 14–42) is used by Jane Austen to expose her deficiencies. Primarily, it is Lucy's language which gives her away. As Austen has remarked, however earnestly she tries, Lucy cannot conceal her lack of education and her ill-breeding. Her ungrammatical and vulgar constructions in lines 14, 20 and 42, combined with colloquialisms (lines 30–33) indicate a corresponding mental sloppiness. Look at the length of Lucy's speech in comparison with Elinor's. It is over-long and sometimes tautologous. In line 36, for instance, the phrase 'in my mind' is unnecessary. Lucy is self-aware and self-pitying. Note the number of times she uses the first person 'I' and 'me' as compared with Elinor's more objective and neutral tone. To an eighteenth-century reader, Lucy's language would stand out as being far too familiar for the circumstances, bearing in mind that she hardly knows Elinor. The personal nature of her comments and the disloyalty to her sister in lines 25–35 transgress the limits of social courtesy and presume an intimacy with Elinor that is unwarranted, while the directness of her question in her next speech, 'What would you do yourself?' is positively indelicate.

Throughout the passage, Jane Austen has Lucy adopt the pose of a heroine from sentimental literature, self-dramatising and using inappropriately extravagant language. 'I only wonder that I am alive' (line 37) and 'I am sure I wonder my heart is not quite broke' (line 42) are just two instances of the linguistic excesses that she favours, but these become more pronounced as the scene continues. Lucy is trying to build up a picture of herself as an isolated, helpless figure, suffering because of her love for Edward and desperately seeking a friend in whom she can confide. But there are inconsistencies in the speech that suggest that her expressions of love are merely a posture. First, the words and phrases that she uses to describe her feelings are trite and secondhand, culled from the cheap romances of the period. This reliance on overworked diction recurs in subsequent speeches, where in addition Lucy is highly repetitive. The phrase 'I dare say' occurs twice in two lines (94 and 96) and in her final outburst the repetition of 'comfort' and 'picture' draws attention to her lack of inventiveness and originality of mind. Further, her pose of emotional delicacy just does not fit with the gross remarks about her sister, nor with the conventional formality of standard phrases, such as 'in the present case' (lines 21 and 22). This confusion of linguistic registers which becomes more pronounced as Lucy continues speaking creates a sense of moral confusion too. Not only is Lucy's language a mark of her intellectual limitations, but Jane Austen also makes it work as a sort of moral barometer.

As the scene develops, we can see how Jane Austen intersperses the dialogue with succinct comments in her own voice that deliberately undercut Lucy's pretentiousness. In lines 43–47, the dispassionate way in which she describes Lucy's actions stresses the external aspects of her behaviour and implies that it is consciously calculated. Note how Jane Austen avoids telling us that Lucy weeps: she merely says that she goes through the motions associated with weeping. Similarly, the word 'carelessly' in line 93 is at odds with the studied way she produces the letter, and the effect is intentionally reductive. This interplay of tones helps to create the comedy of the episode, but also controls the sympathies of the reader, by distancing Lucy and identifying with Elinor. For Jane Austen's technique here moves between the ironic observation of Lucy's artificiality and hard *sense* to a more subtle psychological method of presenting Elinor's *sensibility*. Essentially, the transition is that between eighteenth- and nineteenth-century fictional methods in the movement that takes place from the field of exterior to interior action.

We can see this movement first in Elinor's answer to Lucy in lines 73–7. The spoken words are concise, but we are made privy to Elinor's thoughts which continue via her inward recollections. Access to Elinor's consciousness is extended in lines 98–110 where Jane Austen uses free indirect discourse to dramatise Elinor's mental processes. The italicised '*was*' (line 98) places us directly in Elinor's mind, although Jane Austen maintains the form of third person narrative. The second sentence beginning 'The picture . . .' is lengthy, quite unlike Elinor's normally precise and careful constructions, and gives us a much more subjective view of the logical stages her thoughts are working through. As she becomes more emotional, the syntactic structure breaks down – note the dash in line 105. Jane Austen is cleverly moving us, as readers here, in and out of Elinor's perception. The 'she could hardly stand' for instance is the author's reportage of events, but the very next phrase 'exertion was indispensably necessary' is representing the situation from Elinor's view. The effect of this is to make Elinor both more sympathetic and more psychologically convincing than Lucy. Silence is re-created as an active rather than passive medium, and we are made aware of the existence of a turbulent emotional life beneath the calm manner. Note too the implications of 'for the time' in line 109. Jane Austen wants to make it clear that Elinor's control over her feelings is only temporary. This is reinforced by the emphatic final sentence of the chapter, with its equal stress on 'think' and 'wretched'.

As the scene switches from Lucy to Elinor and back again, we are presented with a variety of ironic contrasts. All Lucy's remarks are purposefully directed. She acts the part of a desolate love-lorn girl only in order to establish her claim on Edward. She takes care to tell Elinor that Edward's letter 'filled the sheet' (line 96), and it is cheering to see that Elinor does not completely lose her own sense of verbal asperity. Her remark to Lucy in line 83 that Edward was particularly depressed 'when he first arrived' from Longstaple counters Lucy's implication in line 68 that it was leaving her that made him sad. There is an active sub-text in operation here and Elinor shows that she can give as good as she gets in implying that it was being at Barton in *her* company which revived him.

The theatricality of Lucy's behaviour makes us rethink our definition of romantic sensibility. Her rhetorical style in, for instance, her repeated use of 'so', her sentimental excesses of 'poor fellow', 'poor Edward', her appeals to her audience via direct questions, her use of props, with the prepared production of the letter and the reference to the ring – all these are reinforced by Jane Austen's aside, 'taking a letter from her pocket' (line 92) in the style of a stage direction. Austen brutally deflates literary sentiment by exposing Lucy, who makes herself out to be a model heroine figure, as a hollow sham. The myth of romance takes on quite a different appearance when it is transferred to the world of social realities in the shape of the ambitious, money-grabbing Lucy Steele.

One final point worth mentioning about this passage is the weight given to Edward's letter. Elinor accepts it as definite proof of an engagement. This has obvious repercussions when we think of the significance attached to the letters Marianne writes to Willoughby. It also suggests the misleading nature of concrete evidence, for although the letter does substantiate the fact of an engagement, it does not prove the existence of affection. The entire scene, down to the fine details, thus forms a disquisition on the deceptive nature of appearances, and the vexed relation between feeling and action.

6 CRITICAL RECEPTION

6.1 CONTEMPORARY VIEWS

Sense and Sensibility was the first of Jane Austen's novels to be published. It was advertised in the *Morning Chronicle* on 31 October 1811 as a 'New Novel by a Lady ————' and came out in November, approximately fifteen years after Jane Austen had begun writing it. The first edition of one thousand copies, priced at fifteen shillings each, was printed at Jane Austen's own expense, a fairly usual practice for a publisher of that time to adopt when he did not want to take risks with a totally unknown author. That Jane Austen was prepared to pay for its publication indicates that she was keen for her work to reach a wider audience than just her own family and a few close friends. Her confidence in herself was justified, for in July 1813, she was able to write 'that every copy of *S and S* is sold, and that it has brought me £140, besides the copyright, if that should ever be of any value.' A second edition was duly prepared for the market and was ready by November.

The first reviews of the book were modestly approving, but critical reviews of fiction in the early nineteenth century did not carry the same status that we attach to them today. The reviewers of *Sense and Sensibility* followed the then normal pattern of paraphrasing the plot, with one or two illustrative excerpts from the text to give potential readers a taste of what they were likely to find. Mainly they remarked on the book's educational merit, as well as noting its capacity to amuse. 'It furnishes a most excellent lesson to young ladies to curb that violent sensibility which too often leads to misery and always to inconvenience and ridicule,' went the report in the *Critical Review* in February 1812, while the notice in the *British Critic* in May was along similar lines. 'Female readers . . . may peruse these volumes not only with satisfaction but with real benefits, for they may learn from them; if they please, many sober and salutary maxims for the conduct of life, exemplified in a very pleasing and entertaining narrative.' It is somewhat ironic that *Sense and Sensibility*, which is in many ways so innovatory, should have found approval as the sort of conventional conduct book it was partly satirising.

Although her work was not granted the sort of critical acclaim we give it now – that was only to come a long time after her death – Jane Austen's novels were immediately recognised as being superior to those of her contemporaries. We get some indication of the general quality of popular fiction that was being churned out by women writers of the time from the satire in *Sense and Sensibility* itself, and clearly her work was in a different class from this. The first serious judgement on her calibre as an artist came in 1816 from Sir Walter Scott, himself a well-known and highly respected author. In a lengthy essay, he commented on her realism as distinguishing her from the approach of earlier romances, and, in pointing out the technical difficulties involved in the realist mode, he showed how Jane Austen's work, by recreating the impression 'of ordinary life' represented what has been termed as a turning point in literary history.

For most nineteenth-century readers, however, the novels of Jane Austen were not regarded very highly. Her subject was too slender for popular taste and although her gift for comic characterisation was appreciated, her work did not conform to the Victorian love of large-scale epic fictions. In a letter written in 1850, the novelist Charlotte Brontë said of Jane Austen,

She does her business of delineating the surface of the lives of genteel English people curiously well; there is a Chinese fidelity, a miniature delicacy in her painting; she ruffles her reader by nothing vehement, disturbs him by nothing profound: the Passions are perfectly unknown to her;

Like other readers of her time, Charlotte Brontë was disappointed by Jane Austen's apparent narrowness of scope and what she felt was a failure to look beyond the superficialities of daily existence.

So although *Sense and Sensibility* with Jane Austen's other books was still in print in the middle of the century – it was re-issued in 1833 as no. 23 in Bentley's series of *Standard Novels* – we can see from Charlotte Brontë's comments how easily its insights could be overlooked. The critic, George Lewes, in an essay in 1859, re-appraising Jane Austen's position, remarked sadly on the general neglect of her work. 'Miss Austen? Oh, yes; she translates from the German, doesn't she?' was, he noted, a 'not uncommon question' in mid-century.

In 1870, Jane Austen's nephew, James Edward Austen-Leigh, published a *Memoir* of his aunt which revived interest in her writing. Yet in describing his 'dear Aunt Jane', Austen-Leigh created what we now see as a misleading portrait of her as a quiet, precise, affectionate woman, good at needlework and at telling fairy-tales, and with a quirky and charming sense of humour. This was the picture of Jane Austen which was to persist in the minds of general readers well into the twentieth century.

The most important departure from this view came in an article which appeared in 1870 following the *Memoir*, written by a renowned Shakespearean scholar, Richard Simpson. In a most penetrating essay, Simpson pointed out that Jane Austen's writing was inspired by her critical faculty and that a tough irony was the cornerstone of her method. *Sense and Sensibility* worked by the 'indirect method of imitating and exaggerating the faults of her models'. Simpson recognised how different Jane Austen was from her contemporaries who copied earlier literary forms without questioning them. He noted the significance of the book's title in its establishment of contrasts crucial to the organisation of the work, and picked up too the centrality of love as a theme and the seriousness with which it is treated. The picture of Jane Austen that Simpson draws is in fact a very modern one: not the withdrawn, genteel amateur, but a conscious artist, actively immersed in the philosophies of her day, intelligent and deeply critical of her own society. His approach to criticism was also very modern, for he saw her as an artist whose growing maturity could be traced by examining the relationships between her earlier and later novels.

6.2 MODERN VIEWS

This view was not to be so wholeheartedly endorsed again until the publication of Mary Lascelles' *Jane Austen and her Art* in 1939, and later in a series of articles in *Scrutiny*, a scholarly journal. Mary Lascelles placed Jane Austen firmly within a literary tradition, demolishing once and for all the image of her that had stuck in the minds of many readers as the amused observer of human follies, sheltered from the harshness of life. Lascelles drew on the reading that Jane Austen had access to and suggested her familiarity with the intellectual debates and problems of her age. *Sense and Sensibility* particularly is a novel that benefits from being seen in such a context, for unless we understand that the novel is in part a response to current theories, we miss its ironic point. Lascelles subjected the novels to a process of in-depth analysis, and convincingly argued that Jane Austen was a thoughtful and accomplished technician with a supreme control over her medium. It is from this point of recognition of her genius that most subsequent appreciation of Jane Austen's work springs. While Jane Austen's reputation has risen steadily over the last forty years, so that most readers now acknowledge the positive qualities of her achievement, *Sense and Sensibility* has probably been the least favourite of her books. 'Grey and cool', was one critic's unenthusiastic opinion, while another has spoken of its 'obvious artistic limitations', the 'mediocre heroes', Edward Ferrars and Colonel Brandon, and the 'wretched episode' of Eliza Williams. Others have complained that the novel overall is too schematic, and the ending unsatisfactory with Jane Austen condemning Marianne to a boring and conventional marriage, 'her energy stifled to the overriding geometry'. The book has also been criticised for being uneven in its blending of comic and serious elements. One persistent difficulty seems to be the question of our responses to the central figures. Where do our sympathies lie – with Elinor or Marianne? Some critics have found the uncertainty a major flaw. Feeling that Elinor is meant to be the novel's true heroine, they have been disturbed to find that Marianne emerges as the more compelling and attractive character.

Marvin Mudrick in a perceptive study of the novels, *Jane Austen, Irony as Defense and Discovery* (1952), argued persuasively that Marianne's position in the text highlights, albeit unconsciously, Jane Austen's ironic methods.

> Against her own moral will and conscious artistic purpose, the creator makes her creation wholly sympathetic – because, one must conclude, Marianne represents an unacknowledged depth of her author's spirit. Still, because it is an aspect which even outside herself, Jane Austen will not acknowledge to be good, Marianne must be humiliated and destroyed.

In this early novel, Mudrick suggests, Jane Austen is not fully in control of her material. Marianne's vitality indicates a split between Jane Austen's emotional sympathy and her moral judgement, and the book's ironic tone, he concludes, is a defensive mechanism, for 'through the flagrant inconsistency of her heroine, Jane Austen is herself revealed in a posture of yearning for the impossible and lost, the passionate and beautiful hero, the absolute lover'.

It is this dilemma about how to read the central antithesis of the book which has aroused most critical interest, and as the arguments and disagreements have mounted, the novel's complexity has become more apparent. One view, for instance, is that Elinor and Marianne dramatise a moral argument, of prudence versus impulsiveness, and that Elinor's triumph is evidence of a clear didactic intention on Jane Austen's part. Alternatively, if the book is viewed in the light of Jane Austen's whole career, the two sisters can be seen as the first example of the dualism of the pairs of young women we find in the later novels and, it has been suggested, the two characters embody differing aspects of a total personality. Yet another valuable approach is a historical one, which shows how the interest in literary parody and the use of certain popular fictional conventions place Jane Austen firmly within the cultural traditions of her day. Increasingly twentieth-century criticism has argued that *Sense and Sensibility* reveals a deeply serious and passionate side to Jane Austen's art. Tony Tanner (1969), for example, recognising, like Mudrick, the power of Marianne's suffering, has interpreted it quite differently. His comment that 'there is a muffled scream from Marianne at the heart of the novel', is used to make a social point. 'The sisters,' he says, 'seem to project some basic division or rift in civilisation as Jane

Austen knew it', and the motifs of sense and sensibility for him are thus seen as reflecting incompatible aspects of social experience.

A development of this line of enquiry which has gained much credibility recently is the feminist approach to the novel. This sees the author's gender as a crucial factor in determining her style and methods of writing. Instead of believing, like Mudrick, that the novel is unconsciously flawed, feminist critics present Jane Austen as deliberately employing techniques that in themselves suggest dissension from a male tradition of writing. In this light, *Sense and Sensibility* appears as a book that above all illuminates the problems faced by unprotected women in an antagonistic society which favours men. The near-tragic tone that seems to disturb the comic texture indicates the tragic possibilities of women's lives, and Marianne's reductive dismissal at the end of the story, instead of being thought an artistic failure, can be seen as representative of the fate of many women of the time, whose only route to survival was through a crushing of their real energies and personalities.

What emerges most forcefully from all of this is the impression that *Sense and Sensibility* continues to evade precise definition. It refuses to fit neatly into any one critical category, although all the above interpretations offer their own valuable and often provocative insights. It remains perhaps Jane Austen's most puzzling book. Laurence Lerner (1967), called it one of the 'most powerful and disturbing of the novels'. Virginia Woolf (1923), said of Jane Austen that 'of all greater writers she is the most difficult to catch in the act of greatness'. Careful reading of *Sense and Sensibility* would seem still to endorse this view.

REVISION QUESTIONS

1. Almost all Jane Austen's novels contain a significant journey. How far do you feel that the move of Elinor and Marianne to London extends the scope of *Sense and Sensibility*?

2. Jane Austen's original title for this novel was *Elinor and Marianne*. What is the effect of the change of title to its present form, *Sense and Sensibility*?

3. Do you think that by limiting herself to a study of 'three or four families', Jane Austen restricts her view of society unnaturally? Can you think of any advantages in concentrating on this fairly narrow field?

4. In another of Jane Austen's novels, a character says, 'Follies and nonsense, whims and inconsistencies, *do* divert me, I own, and I laugh at them whenever I can.' Can you comment on the objects of Jane Austen's mockery in *Sense and Sensibility*, and on the techniques she employs to make them comic?

5. To what extent does *Sense and Sensibility* form a critique of a materialist society?

6. Take any two short contrasting passages from the text (e.g. one dialogue and one commentary), and through a close analysis of the language employed, consider different ways in which irony works in this novel.

7. Consider the ending of *Sense and Sensibility*. Is, as has been suggested, Jane Austen unfair to Marianne? Does she diminish her by the reductive ending? How important is the ending in determining our response to the text as a whole?

8. One critic has said recently that *Sense and Sensibility* is a story of 'female dispossession'. From your reading of the novel, do you think that Jane Austen saw women as particularly disadvantaged members of her society?

9. How do the motifs of language and silence operate in *Sense and Sensibility*?

10. 'Pictures of perfection . . . make me sick and wicked', wrote Jane Austen in a letter to her sister. Would you agree that the 'imperfect' Marianne is more attractive than the 'perfect' Elinor? Why should this be so?

11. In *Sense and Sensibility*, Jane Austen is in part questioning the scope and methods of fiction itself. How do you think she does this? Consider, for example, the terms 'hero' and 'heroine' in this context.

12. Comment on the blending of serious and comic elements in *Sense and Sensibility*.

13. How far would you agree that 'by its very nature *Sense and Sensibility* is unremittingly didactic'?

14. Clearly not all the characters in *Sense and Sensibility* are paid the same degree of attention. Can you see any reason for including the following: Mr and Mrs Palmer, Sir John and Lady Middleton, Anne Steele, Margaret Dashwood, Robert Ferrars?

15. 'To be so bent on Marriage – to pursue a Man merely for the sake of situation – is a sort of thing that shocks me,' wrote Jane Austen. Is this view endorsed in *Sense and Sensibility*?

16. From your reading of *Sense and Sensibility*, how far would you agree with Charlotte Brontë's view that Jane Austen 'ruffles her reader by nothing vehement, disturbs him by nothing profound'?

FURTHER READING

Christopher Gillie, *A Preface to Jane Austen* (London: Longman, 1974).

Barbara Hardy, *A Reading of Jane Austen* (London: Peter Owen, 1975).

Mary Lascelles, *Jane Austen and her Art* (Oxford: Oxford University Press, 1939).

Marghanita Laski, *Jane Austen and her World* (London: Thames and Hudson, 1969).

David Monaghan (ed.), *Jane Austen in a Social Context* (London: Macmillan, 1981).

Norman Page, *The Language of Jane Austen* (Oxford: Basil Blackwell, 1972).

LeRoy W. Smith, *Jane Austen and the Drama of Women* (London: Macmillan, 1983).

Brian Southam (ed.), *Sense and Sensibility, Pride and Prejudice, and Mansfield Park: Casebook Series* (London: Macmillan, 1976).

Tony Tanner, *Jane Austen* (London: Macmillan, 1986).

Mastering English Literature
Richard Gill

Mastering English Literature will help readers both to enjoy English Literature and to be successful in 'O' levels, 'A' levels and other public exams. It is an introduction to the study of poetry, novels and drama which helps the reader in four ways – by providing ways of approaching literature, by giving examples and practice exercises, by offering hints on how to write about literature, and by the author's own evident enthusiasm for the subject. With extracts from more than 200 texts, this is an enjoyable account of how to get the maximum satisfaction out of reading, whether it be for formal examinations or simply for pleasure.

Work Out English Literature ('A' level)
S.H. Burton

This book familiarises 'A' level English Literature candidates with every kind of test which they are likely to encounter. Suggested answers are worked out step by step and accompanied by full author's commentary. The book helps students to clarify their aims and establish techniques and standards so that they can make appropriate responses to similar questions when the examination pressures are on. It opens up fresh ways of looking at the full range of set texts, authors and critical judgements and motivates students to know more of these matters.